MEET
CALVIN COOLIDGE
The Man Behind the Myth

MEET
CALVIN COOLIDGE
The Man Behind the Myth

EDITED BY
Edward Connery Lathem

The Stephen Greene Press

BRATTLEBORO, VERMONT

1960

ACKNOWLEDGMENTS

The editor's first expression of thanks is due, and gladly tendered, Mr. and Mrs. John Coolidge for their innumerable kindnesses and unceasing helpfulness. To Mrs. Myrtie C. Lathem, Mrs. Inez M. Kellam, and Mrs. Claire B. Packard, each of whom had a large part in the preparation of this collection, the editor is much indebted. To other individuals who graciously gave both assistance and encouragement he is also most grateful, as well as to several libraries, most notably the Forbes Library of Northampton, Massachusetts, and its librarian, Mr. Lawrence E. Wikander.

The selections that constitute this volume are from writings published at various times over a period of many years. Appreciative acknowledgment is made to the individuals and publishers who have generously granted permission for the inclusion, in full or in extract, of various sections of text. Reference is made to the following sources:

"Calvin Coolidge—After 20 Years" by Alfred Pearce Dennis, *The Saturday Evening Post*, September 20, 1924; copyright, 1924, by The Curtis Publishing Company. Frank W. Stearns' letter of August 16, 1916, the text of which is taken from the copy in the possession of the recipient, Mr. Robert W. Maynard. *Concentrated New England* by Kenneth Roberts; copyright, 1924, by The Bobbs-Merrill Company. "The Genius of the Average" by Gamaliel Bradford, *The Atlantic Monthly*, January 1930; copyright, 1929, by The Atlantic Monthly Company. "Who Made Coolidge?" by Frank W. Buxton, *The Boston Herald*, September 14, 1923. An appraisal of Calvin Coolidge by H. L. Mencken, *The American Mercury*, April 1933; copyright, 1933, by The American Mercury, Inc. "Puritanism de Luxe in the Coolidge Era" by Walter Lippmann, *Vanity Fair*, May 1926, as reprinted in *Men of Destiny;* book copyright, 1927, by The Macmillan Company. A brief passage from volume two of *Memoirs* by Herbert Hoover (to accompany an earlier quotation published elsewhere); copyright, 1951, 1952, by Herbert Hoover. "The Real Calvin Coolidge," a series of articles edited by Grace Coolidge (including articles by Bertrand H. Snell, Ercole Cartotto, Bernard M. Baruch, Mrs. Dwight W. Morrow, John T. Lambert, Will Rogers, Ralph W. Hemenway, John Q. Tilson, Charles A. Andrews), *Good Housekeeping*, February-June 1935; copyright, 1935, by International Magazine Company, Inc. *Starling of the White House* by Edmund W. Starling; copyright, 1946, by Simon and Schuster, Inc. *"Dear Mr. President . . ."* by Ira R. T. Smith; copyright, 1949, by Ira R. T. Smith. "A Week in the White House with President Coolidge" by French Strother, *The World's Work*, November 1923; copyright, 1923, by Doubleday, Page & Company. "Presidents and First Ladies" (part two) by Mary Randolph, *Ladies Home Journal*, June 1936; copyright, 1936, by The Curtis Publishing Company. "Aide to Four Presidents" by Wilson Brown, *American Heritage*, February 1955; copyright, 1955, by American Heritage Publishing Company, Inc. *The Star-Spangled Manner* by Beverley Nichols (London: Jonathan Cape, 1928). "When Cal Coolidge Came to Visit Us" by William J. Bulow, *The Saturday Evening Post*, January 4, 1947; copyright, 1947, by The Curtis Publishing Company. *Portrait and Pageant* by Frank O. Salisbury (London: John Murray, 1944). "Mr. Coolidge's State Papers. . ." by Mark Sullivan, the *New York Herald Tribune*, March 3, 1929; copyright, 1929, by New York Tribune, Inc. A passage from *As I Knew Them* by James E. Watson; copyright, 1936, by The Bobbs-Merrill Company. A series of articles by F. W. Plummer, *The Boston Globe*, May 18-24, 1930; copyright, 1930, by Globe Newspaper Company. "The Calvin Coolidge Nobody Knew" by Herman Beaty, *Hearst's International-Cosmopolitan*, April 1933; copyright, 1933, by International Magazine Company, Inc. "Back in Ward Four" by Bruce Barton, *The American Magazine*, March 1931; copyright, 1931, by The Crowell Publishing Company. "Last Letters of Calvin Coolidge" by Everett Sanders, *The Saturday Evening Post*, March 25, 1933; copyright, 1933, by The Curtis Publishing Company. "I Do Not Fit in with These Times" by Henry L. Stoddard, the New York *Sun*, January 6, 1933 (as reprinted in pamphlet form). "Death of Mr. Coolidge," *The New York Times*, January 6, 1933; copyright, 1933, by The New York Times Company. An appraisal of Calvin Coolidge by Alfred E. Smith, *New Outlook*, February 1933; copyright, 1933, by Outlook Publishing Company, Inc. *In the Green Mountain Country* by Clarence Day, originally published in the New York *American* and reprinted in 1934, with acknowledgment, by Yale University Press. The photograph on the spine of the Jacket is by Underwood & Underwood News Photos, Inc.

E. C. L.

Contents

Introduction

HIS WAS a career well seasoned with paradox. That a man so quiet, so introspective, so taciturn, so completely lacking in the expansive, outgoing, voluble qualities ordinarily thought to characterize the politician, should have achieved any success at all in seeking public office, to say nothing of having attained during a quarter century of orderly upward progression the Presidency of the United States, was in itself gigantically incredible: one of the basic paradoxes of the Coolidge story. But the crowning paradox of all was to come at the end of his career, as he turned from the glitter and grandeur of official Washington to take up private life once more.

Few of our Presidents have left office enjoying so ample a measure of popular acclaim as did Calvin Coolidge on the fourth of March, 1929. And it was a popularity by no means restricted to members of his own party or supporters of his political principles and policies. "One cannot remark the going of Mr. Coolidge without a certain regret," declared one of the nation's leading magazines as his term neared its close, "a regret that has nothing to do with his qualities as a public man, one that is purely personal. Mr. Coolidge is a character; he has a pungency and flavor that most public men lack. Even if one does not admire, one cannot help having a certain liking for him."

Nearly a decade earlier, Bruce Barton, in one of the first major articles about Coolidge to appear in a publication of national circulation, had written, "We like novelties, we Americans; especially do we like them in our public life—and nowhere else are we offered so pathetically few of them. Year after year the same familiar types crop up in politics to go through the same threadbare

1

campaign gymnastics. . . . Only at rare intervals does something fresh and new and different break across the dull horizon; and when that unexpected does occur, we draw a deep breath, and thank God and take courage."

Theodore Roosevelt had been one such "blessed phenomenon"; Woodrow Wilson another. "And now," Barton declared, "to stir our jaded interest another new thing under the sun has appeared— a politician who apparently conforms to none of the established rules; who operates after his own peculiar fashion, and yet somehow succeeds in getting his fellow citizens to vote for him in numbers that have made all political observers stop, look, and listen."

Mr. Coolidge was then still Governor of Massachusetts, but the Boston Police Strike had, overnight, made him famous. "The Silent Man on Beacon Hill" had seized the nation's fancy with his bold assertion, "There is no right to strike against the public safety. . . ." He was looked upon as "a sentinel of law and order," and there was talk of him in connection with even higher elective office—in connection with the Presidency itself.

Although earnestly sought for him by his supporters, the Republican Presidential nomination was, nonetheless, to be denied Coolidge at the Chicago convention in 1920. His potential strength lay principally with the ordinary delegates and not with the political leaders, at least some of whom considered the self-contained, undemonstrative Yankee to be "the coldest proposition in modern politics." When the forces of Wood and Lowden, the leading contenders of the first day's balloting, were found to be in hopeless deadlock, a council of party chieftains deftly sank their tomahawks into the hopes of all other aspirants, Governor Coolidge among them, and powwowed a handsome, tractable brave of the Senatorial tribe, Warren Gamaliel Harding, into the first-place candidacy. The Senate sachems could, however, but watch with impatient surprise and ill-conceived dismay as the convention suddenly took back into its own hands the naming of a running mate. With a rush and a roar the deed was done, and Calvin Coolidge was designated Vice-Presidential nominee.

What a dissimilar pair they were, Coolidge and Harding! More than just opposite, they seemed in fact contradictory in both personality and nature. It was almost as if fate had conspired to provide for the warm, jovial, effusive Ohioan a complete antithesis in the person of his second. An easy victory, at any rate, was theirs at the polls. (It was, as someone quipped, a year of "kangaroo tickets": Harding and Coolidge against Cox and Franklin Roosevelt; in both cases, "back legs stronger than the front.")

When, in 1921, Calvin Coolidge arrived in Washington to take up the duties of his new office he was regarded by the inhabitants of that "City of Conversation" as "perhaps the oddest and most singular apparition this vocal and articulate settlement has ever known." He was "a well of silence," a "center of stillness." Nobody quite understood him, this Vermont-born, Amherst-educated, small-city lawyer—shy, uncommunicative, aloof—who somehow or other, by means inexplicable and for reasons incomprehensible, had climbed the political ladder so skillfully, so unfalteringly; who over all the years had experienced but a single defeat at the hands of the public.

"In common with everyone else at Washington, I have been eager," wrote one prominent journalist some six months after the new Vice-President's advent at the Capital, "to pluck out the heart of Mr. Coolidge's mystery, to discover what sort of man he is, to establish a basis for appraisal. All in vain, for he has revealed nothing, disclosed nothing." Surely, however, such a situation could not long continue; he could not indefinitely evade the searching scrutiny now so intently fixed upon him; he would not escape a final and comprehensive evaluation.

"Before the microscopists at Washington are done with him," the writer over-confidently predicted, "he will be catalogued and indexed and cross-referenced." Few prophecies have gone wider of the mark, for Washington with all its cleverness and acuity never did "get" Calvin Coolidge, either during his two and a half years as Vice-President or later.

When, at Harding's death, he was suddenly installed as the nation's Chief Executive, the puzzle of Calvin Coolidge became all the more nettlesome to those dedicated to solving "The Great Coolidge Mystery," to charting the contours of the country's "Grand Enigma." And if these explorers were confounded in their attempts to measure and define Mr. Coolidge, they were baffled also by a realization, slowly arrived at, that somehow or other the frustrating object of their investigation was being astoundingly successful in projecting himself to the people:

"Political Washington," recorded one observer less than a year after Mr. Coolidge had been called to the Presidency, "has at last awakened to the fact that President Coolidge is getting an immense and increasing backing from the American public. The recognition of this rather amazing phenomenon is grudging and reluctant, to be sure, and tinged with a sort of blinking incredulity, but it can no longer be overlooked. . . .

"Acceptance of Mr. Coolidge as a power in himself, apart from his office, has been the slower because it has been so utterly unexpected. It violates almost all notions of what a man should be and do to win public favor. It flies in the face of every political rule of thumb. There were, indeed, some who, when President Harding died, did hope that Mr. Coolidge would 'develop qualities of leadership,' but comparatively few believed that he could, and almost none suspected that just as he was, with his known character of caution, calmness, silence, and retirement, he could become a dominant figure. He has not changed, he has shown little of what is usually considered leadership, yet his strength is as unmistakable as it is surprising. . . ."

But public favor is, of course, a fickle thing; and the question remained, Would this great popularity continue? Would it last to the next election? Last it assuredly did, and Coolidge, integrity unchallenged, still possessing an undiminished public confidence even in the wake of the scandals of his predecessor's administration, smashingly carried the 1924 Presidential contest with a huge majority. Beyond this, his astonishing popularity continued, ever mounting.

He was known to the public as few men ever have been known: his sharply chiseled features, his wiry frame, his outward characteristics and highly individual traits. With a familiarity born of affection the nation called him "Cal" and delighted in the telling and re-telling of countless "Coolidge stories," as it fondly mimicked his nasal twang and Yankee manner of speech.

He stood in bold outline as the unmistakable symbol of an era—assuredly more by contrast than through any personification of its more typical features, but its symbol nevertheless—an era that was to depart with him and the exact like of which, as with the man himself, the country can never experience again.

When, in 1929, having *chosen* not to run for re-election, he quietly gave up occupancy of the White House to his successor and returned again to the Northampton duplex that had been his home for so many years, he was the object of an all-but-unprecedented national regard. Yet comprehended he was not! Though universally known and warmly acclaimed, he remained to the end—tauntingly, bafflingly—"Public Puzzle No. 1."

"Is Mr. Coolidge," asked one editor, "a uniquely dull case of a political accident who knew enough to steer a middle course and keep his teeth together, or is he, as we begin to suspect, the ultimate extension of Yankee hoss-trading sagacity, the apotheosis of non-committal prudence and straw-colored good sense?"

Thus, here at its close was to be found the grand, climactic paradox of Calvin Coolidge's career. Notwithstanding his height of popularity, he left the Presidency as he had entered upon it, an inscrutable enigma, unfathomed and seemingly unfathomable.

Across the years, in retrospect, it becomes increasingly plain that any real understanding of Calvin Coolidge by most of his contemporaries was largely prevented by the myth that early grew up around him. The myth was, to be sure, based upon the reality of the man, but it presented him in caricature rather than in realistic form—a verbal caricature that portrayed its subject by selective concentration on only certain of the more prominent features of his character, his personality, and manner—a representation achieved through simplification and subordination, through magnification and distortion. The result, like all successful products of the art whether written or drawn, was a vivid, immediately recognizable picture, but a delineation not to be accepted as a close and faithful likeness or anything other than a clever exaggeration, an amusing travesty.

This mythical misrepresentation, which in all its parts came to be so rapturously applauded by the American public, may have had its beginnings in the period of Mr. Coolidge's rise in municipal and state politics back home in Massachusetts, but it was given its real substance, form, and color by the members of Washington's press corps when he emerged upon the national scene as Vice-President. Part, perhaps, of the reason that the Capital newsmen set down such a fanciful record of the man was that they really viewed him as but a quaint figure who failed to fit into any of the usual Washington stereotypes and who somehow couldn't be adequately defined in terms of realistic expression. Moreover, the new occupant of the Vice-Presidency so scrupulously avoided making headlines of any sort for himself that the reporters assigned to provide Vice-Presidential "coverage" were hard pressed to produce column inches for public consumption save by concentrating on the personality and character of their subject. With bold strokes and exercising ample artistic license, they thus "created" their stories and along with them the montage that became the myth.

The elements of this "Coolidge myth" were many: dramatic over-statements of fundamental truths. Chief among them, for example, was that based upon Mr. Coolidge's retiring nature and fundamental taciturnity. This was the reality, the genuine condition; but as an ingredient of the myth these qualities were transformed into something a good deal more than shyness and "adequate brevity." The Coolidge silence became a conspicuous ingredient of the nation's social environment, and thousands of inches of newspaper space were devoted to describing it, often in terms of gentle, good-hearted burlesque. It was reported that he could be silent in five different languages, that he used words only as a last resort, that when on rare occasion he did open his mouth moths flew out. The fact that if he wished to do so Mr. Coolidge could talk as freely as the next fellow, that at times he was in actuality nearly as garrulous as a magpie, had no effect whatever on the public's fondly held, romantically cherished notion of their Chief Executive as "Calvin the Silent."

He practiced the virtues of New England frugality. In the mythical reflection he became a dour, closefisted "national pinchpenny," the subject of a vast repertory of jokes on Coolidge "tightness." That he splendidly declared he favored economy not to save money but to save people was, by and large, considered prosaically irrelevant; and it was rated a wonderfully funny proposal when on the eve of his leaving the Presidency someone facetiously suggested he be sent to Scotland to give a course in thrift at the University of Aberdeen. Even Mr. Coolidge himself, it is recorded, was amused.

He was a man of serious disposition and impassive façade, but the myth made him stolid and morose; and someone jokingly reported that when he did smile, "the effect was like ice breaking in a New England river."

He might with careful logic comment on a proposal for war debts cancellation, "The money we furnished we had to borrow. Someone must pay it. It cannot be cancelled. If we do not collect it from Europe, we must collect it from our own taxpayers." Such economic reasoning was considered admirable, but really the people much preferred the laconic response, "Well, they hired the money, didn't they?" The homely maxim was more in keeping with the mythical character they so much enjoyed. And so it was with other matters.

Truly the public fancy was captivated and enthralled. The people rejoiced in this enchanting work of fantasy that had been made for their delectation and were completely disinclined to give up the luxury of something they relished so hugely as they did the "Coolidge myth."

It must not, of course, be supposed that they did not also have a clear awareness of, and regard for, Mr. Coolidge's impressive record of public service, his steady ascent of the political ladder, as rung by rung he climbed to the very height of public responsibility: Councilman, City Solicitor, state Representative, Mayor, member and then President of the state Senate, Lieutenant-Governor, Governor, Vice-President, and, finally, President of the United States. They were conscious, too, that his principal attention throughout had seemed to be intently fixed upon performing the duties of his incumbency and not on anxiously scanning the horizon to discover what course might seem most auspicious to the interests of personal advantage and advancement. Let the office seek the man had been his precept, and he had lived by his own pronouncement that "we need more of the office desk and less of the show window in politics." All in all it was a record that inspired quiet confidence in the quiet man who had created it.

Moreover, the country discovered in Mr. Coolidge many other qualities which, for varying reasons, proved particularly appealing to the America of the 1920's: an impeccable honesty, a refreshing serenity, a remarkable simplicity and humility, an incisive and homely wisdom. At one and the same time, he was thought of as being both a strangely wonderful "green-apple genius" and the incarnation of "the average man"—perhaps, in sum, to be accurately styled an "extraordinary ordinary man."

And how did Mr. Coolidge himself regard the aura of make-believe that so inescapably surrounded him? Ample evidence exists to reveal that at times he actually took a perverse pleasure in some of the features of the myth and to a degree enjoyed, on occasion, assuming the pose of its character.

In an unpublished, off-the-record address made four months after his accession to the Presidency, he once, in whimsical vein, gave voice to his own awareness of both the fantasy and its source:

"I suppose that I am not very good 'copy,' " he remarked at a Gridiron Club Dinner in December, 1923, addressing members of the White House Correspondents Association and their guests. "You know it is the unusual and the extraordinary event that is really a news item. The usual and ordinary man is not the source of very much news. But the boys have been very kind and considerate to me," he chided satirically, referring to the Washington reporters, "and where there has been any discrepancy, they have filled it in and glossed it over, and they have manufactured some.

"They have undertaken to endow me with some characteristics and traits that I didn't altogether know I had. But I have done the best I could to be perfectly fair with them and, in public, to live up to those traits. I have sometimes found it a little difficult, especially under the provocation that arises out of some of the things that I read in the newspapers, but I have been able to contain myself on those occasions." Nonetheless, he puckishly confided, "My fellow countrymen have put me in situations where I have found I could not refrain from speaking."

It is of the order of a myth to enlarge with the years, and in such fashion the "Coolidge myth" grew as his era rushed on precipitously to its close. Then, with the passage of additional time, its outlines and features were somehow to soften, to mellow, to develop into what has at last become a substantial American legend—a legend that today reveals a man part sphinx, part Yankee wizard, and a unique, vastly over-sized third part that is just plain "Cal."

What is to be said by way of a final appraisal of Calvin Coolidge? Is he to be ranked among America's top political leaders—"the Palmerston of our political history," as one of his prominent contemporaries prophesied he would come to be regarded? Or, in the negative extreme, must he be written off as merely a drab, odd, inarticulate little man, a "darling of the gods" who was "pitchforked into the Presidency" and had neither the ability nor the courage to do more than silently and listlessly drift with the tide of affairs—"the nearest thing to nothing," as one editor belligerently labelled him, "we ever had as President."

To resolve any such questions at all adequately would require agreement on the proper criteria for evaluating greatness, success, and failure.

There are those who will urge that few men have more completely measured up to the Emersonian definition that, "He is great who is what he is from Nature, and who never reminds us of others." Some, too, will maintain that he admirably fulfilled, also, the concept of human greatness which emphasizes the happy coincidence of "the man" and "the moment." Others, however, will be less convinced that one can reasonably talk of him and greatness in any context, quoting, perhaps, Stevenson's observation that, "Ice and iron cannot be welded."

Be that as it may, clearly only two kinds of Presidents are ever remembered in after years as anything more than names: those who have held office in stirring times and whose administrations have been associated with important events, and those who endure because of the definite impact of their personality.

Calvin Coolidge was decidedly of the latter class. His was not, in the ordinary sense of the term, a striking personality. It had little of forcefulness and vigor, and its qualities were, perhaps, generally more negative than positive. It contained more firmness than buoyancy, more durability than effervescence, more depth than height. But a vivid personality it was, no less distinct for its special character nor any less enduring.

It is a fact that Mr. Coolidge was not a dynamic, indomitable President who led or drove the country into taking courses of action or assuming positions in which he resolutely believed. Had he been, he probably could have attained neither the office nor the popularity that were his in that particular age, for it is doubtful that the decade of the '20's wanted or would have sanctioned such a man in the White House.

"Surely no one will write of these years since August, 1923," declared Walter Lippmann editorially on the day Mr. Coolidge left office, "that an aggressive President altered the destiny of the Republic. Yet it is an important fact that no one will write of these same years that the Republic wished its destiny to be altered."

Whatever evaluations historians may place upon the political events and activities of Mr. Coolidge's public life, the real and lasting importance of his career lies, in point of fact, in the quiet impress of the man himself upon his countrymen and on the American scene. Through the uniqueness of his character, his personality and manner, and through the elements of the living myth and legend that grew up around him, he has become more than a chapter in the nation's history; he has become, as is a greater immortality, a racy, giddy, pleasing part of America's folklore and heritage. He was, and he continues to be, "Silent Cal," "The Man from Vermont," "Concentrated New England," "A Puritan in Babylon"; the cautious, thrifty, reserved Yankee who presided over a reckless, extravagant, blatant age, who achieved a zenith of popularity and yet who—ironically and paradoxically—was really so little understood.

"He is," it was once remarked in apt and striking metaphor, "a sort of old-fashioned russet apple of the kind that used to grow on all farms: small, dull-colored, harsh-surfaced, but aromatic and savorsome." And the russet, the writer might well have added, was especially prized for its qualities as a particularly "good keeper."

So it has been with Calvin Coolidge. The unusual, tangy flavor of the man has pleased the American palate, and the memory of him continues to be both pungent and unforgettable.

*   *   *

This book does not concern itself with the events of Calvin Coolidge's life, nor does it attempt to document or evaluate the accomplishments of his career. It is not in that sense a biographical work. Rather, its pages are devoted to providing as clear, as intimate, and as vivid as possible a portrayal of the true character and personality of one of the most baffling and enigmatic figures in America's political and social history. Here is presented the thirtieth President of the United States as but few persons ever saw him: the man behind the myth, as known and recorded by those who, in one way or another, were especially close to him and as described and appraised by other astute and perceptive contemporary observers.

EDWARD CONNERY LATHEM

Hanover, New Hampshire
March 1960

I

SPEAKING IN GENERAL

The Man Who Became President

By ALFRED PEARCE DENNIS

Writing in 1924, a year after Calvin Coolidge had succeeded to the Presidency, Alfred Pearce Dennis, who became Vice-Chairman of the U.S. Tariff Commission, recalls his associations with Mr. Coolidge during the period, a quarter of a century earlier, when the future Chief Executive was just beginning his legal and political career and Mr. Dennis himself was a young teacher of history and politics.

WE BOTH started work in Northampton, Massachusetts, in the late '90's, he a fledgling lawyer just out of Amherst, I a professor in Smith College with a few Princeton degrees as an evidence of good faith. We lodged almost within a stone's throw of each other, took our meals together . . . , fought each other tooth and nail politically, respected each other, and occasionally groped around for each other's companionship. . . .

Coolidge shared modest quarters on Round Hill with Rob Weir, steward of the Clarke School. I lodged a little more pretentiously in a mansion at the foot of Round Hill. We frequently fell into step with each other as we started downtown in the morning for the day's work. I have a perfect picture of young Coolidge as he strode down Elm Street some twenty-five years ago. Not a magnetic personality.

Had he been simply mediocre and commonplace, one would have gained no clearer impression of him at all. But just as a man may be so picturesquely ugly as to attract attention, so Coolidge's personality was apparently so arid that it at once challenged human in-

15

terest. In appearance he was splendidly null, apparently deficient in red corpuscles, with a peaked, wire-drawn expression. You felt that he was always about to turn up his coat collar against a chilling east wind. As he walked there was no motion of the body above the waist. The arms hung immobile, with the torso as inflexible as the effigy of a lay figure.

In his enigmatic character he has been compared to the Sphinx. From the enigma standpoint the comparison is inexact; but like the Sphinx, he seemed to look out with unseeing eyes upon a world which held no glow, no surprises. Desert sand blown by the winds, dust—endless, tantalizing dust.

The photographers do him a disservice in softening the lines of his face. The lines are the most characteristic thing about his physiognomy. The tight-lipped mouth was more than a thin line or gash across the face. It dipped in sharp furrows at the corners. One finds the same dip in the jaws of a bulldog or a snapping turtle; creatures that, having taken hold, continue to hold. There are lines of concentration, too, puckering up between the sandy eyebrows, crow's-feet radiating from the corners of the eyes, lines which were born of amusement with the world rather than with the pain of it. He seldom laughed out loud, but a thousand times I have seen him laugh with his eyes. The wrinkles came when he was amused.

As to clothes, he was always well dressed; but he was not what you might call a natty dresser; he was neat, he was inconspicuous. The dean of his wardrobe was a severe, high-crowned derby hat, set on an even keel and never by any chance adjusted to a rakish angle; a serviceable hat withal, doing duty at the golf links as well as on Main Street.

As far as I know, there was no particular call to dress up for any great occasion. He was rarely seen in any Northampton drawing rooms. He simply hadn't the time for it. As mayor, he had the privilege of a free box in the Academy of Music, one of the few municipally run theaters in the world; but he seldom appeared in person as a patron of dramatic art. He liked the theater, but there was always something else that pressed for his attention. . . .

Young Coolidge always appeared to me to have a mighty poor

time in life. Never learned to dance or play cards; music had little appeal for him. He evinced about as much interest in the pretty rosy-cheeked college girls as modern youth would display in a sprinkling of cheap automobiles on the public highway. This was not because he disliked women, but because he was shy. He held women in reverential awe, as mysterious human beings. He was the devotee who worshipped from afar.

Neither in college nor in Northampton did Coolidge ever learn to play. For one thing, he did not have the time, nor, I think, did he have the disposition. We got him to join the Warner Meadow Golf Club, and he struggled to display a little spontaneous interest in the game. I remember so well the observation of a lusty young player who sat weary and dejected on the club veranda. The poor fellow seemed to be all in.

He remarked wearily, "I have just played a round with Cal Coolidge and feel as tired as if I had come in from a twenty-mile hike. He keeps his eye on the ball all the time and tries so hard. It is not that he plays such a rotten game of golf, but that he does not know what play is. He makes work out of it. You may not believe it, but I'd rather play with that old goose hen D_____. He makes me mad, always losing his ball and bellyaching about something, but at least he has a zest for the game."

The love of play was not bred in the Coolidge blood, and he could no more affect to be frolicsome than he could affect to be anything else he was not. Life, I fancy, was pretty sterile of amusements in the Vermont hills fifty years ago. . . .

To many a man life would seem poor, indeed, if uncrowned by the glory of beauty—music, poetry, art, the changing colors on land and sea. Was young Coolidge really blind to beauty, dead to the enchantment of women? Or did he really see life in better perspective than the most of us? Had he something more important to think about? Was he like Saint Bernard, who fared along the shores of lovely Lake Leman with his eyes bent upon the neck of his mule lest his thoughts be diverted from the contemplation of sin, death, and judgment to come by the exquisite beauty of the landscape about him?

One June evening we went trolley riding. There were no automobiles in those days. It was the day after college commencement. One feels let down after such occasions. We scrambled into a front seat, and it was nice and cool bowling along in the open car across green meadows, by the shining river, and then up, up the heights to Mountain Park on the crest of the hills. Within the band played, peanut roasters hissed, humanity giggled and screamed on flying horses and roller coasters. The carnival spirit reigned. No word had been spoken by either of us since we left Northampton. My companion at last broke into speech—"I guess we have had about enough excitement without taking in any shows." So we climbed aboard a returning car.

Speeding homeward, we halted on a turnout to let a south-bound car go by. The five-minute pause in the soft, quiet June night. The dim outlines of the river, the green hills, the grassy meadows bathed in moonlight, the scent of wild grape, the flit of little winged things in the air, faint pipings in the grass, life palpitating about us, a world of beauty—aching beauty. To my stricken fancy, the beauty of the entire universe was symbolized in a slender, *printanière* creature who had appeared the day before in the college graduating class, ethereal, clothed in filmy white raiment with roses in her hands. The very thought of her insulated me entirely from the tediums of a commonplace world. It was my firm intention to seek her out some day, to impress her; yes, I would captivate her by the allure of some fine achievement, by my brilliant talk. A querulously discordant note from my companion jarred me out of the splendid reverie.

"I have been kind of counting up the amount of labor and material such as crossties, rails, poles, copper wire, to say nothing of rolling equipment, that have gone into this line. Some of our folks think we ought to strike for a nickel fare to Mountain Park. It's good politics to agree with 'em, but I can hardly see it that way," he rasped. . . . "Just as a matter of fairness, looks like the road is entitled to a chance to make a living just the same as you and I."

Ye gods, what a man! Brooding over railroad crossties and trolley equipment in moments that should have been dedicated to beauty, mystery, romance.

But the lady of my dreams passed me by in life as Beatrice once passed Dante without speaking. The memory of her faded with the years. Long afterward I met her by chance. Plumpness had descended upon her as lava overwhelms a doomed city upon a fair mountain slope. The springlike quality had entirely evaporated. She of the deliciously baffling reticences had become vocally incessant with the years. My brilliant talk was limited to tepid interjections, "Yes, indeed!" "Oh, really!" Any cretin could have made as good a showing.

Not so long after the Mountain Park excursion the unromantic Coolidge married the most charming girl in town. I remember Grace Goodhue vividly, hardly out of her teens when she came to Northampton to . . . the Clarke School. A creature of spirit, fire, and dew, given to blithe spontaneous laughter, with eager birdlike movements, as natural and unaffected as sunlight or the sea, a soul that renders the common air sweet.

What did she see in him?—everybody asked. Certainly no Prince Charming or knight in shining armor. She saw, let us believe, as by swift divination that unseen thing which we call, for want of a better name, character. As by revelation, she apprehended what had to be beaten into the heads of the rest of us. . . .

It is said of Von Moltke that he could be silent in seven languages. Calvin Coolidge, as I knew him, could at least be silent in one. Fundamentally, his quality of silence was only another phase of his instinct for frugality. The logic is clear enough; a man who is naturally frugal in expenditure, whether for dress, food or amusement, will be frugal in the expenditure of speech.

Mr. Coolidge has always been bashful. This, too, helps to explain his reticences. Though silence may sometimes be an evidence of mental vacuity, there simply being no ideas to express, in the case of Mr. Coolidge silence reflects the habit of concentration. He was always reflecting on something, turning over something in his mind. Considering the awful brevity of human life and the magnitude of the tasks to be accomplished, silence may be employed as a weapon for the conquest of time. It is a short cut to an objective, saving detours. Certainly not a winning, electioneering quality in a back-slapping, declamatory, at-a-boy age. For a great executive, however, silence may serve better than a fatal gift of fluency. . . .

The Coolidge quality of silence unless he had something specific to say had rather a charm for me. It made him easy and comfortable to get along with. You could sit with him on a three-hour train ride from Northampton to Boston and really enjoy his compainionship although he never said a word. With most any other man you would have had the fidgets, the quietness would have become tense. But with him quietness was never assumed; it was as natural as breathing. And the queer part of it is that he was always seeking out companionship even though he did not want to talk. He always seemed to be a lonely man. If there were ten vacant seats in a railroad car, he would walk disconsolately down the aisle, seeking an acquaintance, sidle into the seat with him, and relapse into solemn silence.

There are those in the world who talk and those who get things done. Connor as city solicitor reviewed the year's record of eleven cases in four printed pages of the annual report. This was considered the irreducible minimum of brevity. Coolidge reviewed his year as city solicitor in two pages covering fifteen cases. A man craving the stark truth of things can't be fed with rhetoric and metaphors. He was frugal with adjectives as a miser with money. Such words as "frightfully," "awfully," "splendid," "fascinating," had no more standing with him than if they were alien terms brought over from the Coptic. His speech was about the run of the mill, but shorn of all extravagances and objurgations. Powerful cuss words invoked by politicians as an intellectual means of meeting great crises had no place in the Coolidge vocabulary. He even eschewed the feebler New England diaconal oaths such as "by heck" and "by cracky." He swore not at all. I never heard him tell a vulgar story. He possessed what Jeremy Taylor calls "the prudent endearment of moderate speech."

In speech, as in aught else, there is a strength in moderation. A quiet man with quiet clothes so like the protective coloring of an animal that they merged perfectly with his environment and made no impression upon you whatever. If he took a vacation it was always a quiet vacation. His marriage was described in the local paper as a quiet wedding with no attendants. In the old days all was quiet along the Connecticut just as today all is quiet along the Potomac. Quietude in a clamant world; imperturbability in the turmoil of our great human ant hill. . . .

Coolidge luck! I never observed that he had any particular luck in the eight years I was thrown with him. He worked hard for what he got, and I could not then or since see any broad foundation of his success except the public confidence in him. Now a streak of luck may excite the admiration or even the envy of the public, but not its confidence. The little way in the modest city that saw his success was small. The broad way of his later life that saw his success was great, but the elements which contributed to his success were the same, I think, in all stages of his career. A baseball nine may win a particular contest by breaks in the game, but no team keeps on winning through an entire season and rises to first place in a league merely through luck.

Luck, whether in love, horse racing, stock jobbing or poker playing, does not favor any person consistently when spread over a period of twenty-five years. The law of averages works out whether computed by an insurance actuary or appraised in Emerson's essay on Compensation. Nobody but a savage believes that the destiny of either an individual or a tribe is determined by blind luck.

So it was that I said good-by to Calvin Coolidge one day in front of Kingsley's Northampton drug store. There was almost a trace of warmth in his handshake and nasal benediction, "Luck to you!" That was nineteen years ago. I next saw him in the White House, at the head of his own table, in splendid contrast to the modest little room in Rahar's Inn where we formerly sat at meat together. One might have expected to find him remote, seated in solemn detachment, hinting of mountainous responsibilities, burdened by the importunities of office seekers and the complex problems which would tax the wisdom of Solomon. Not a bit of it. Twenty years of power and place apparently had left no mark upon his manner. He made no reference whatever to anything that had intervened since we last met. He was eager to talk, wanted to tell me all about the changes in Northampton.

"You know Warren died and his livery stable has been moved away from the lot next to the Catholic Church. Professor Emerick's dead, too. Lived across Massasoit Street from me. He left his family better off than we thought. Two of the four Dragon brothers who kept the barber shop are dead, Louie and Ed, but George and Duffy are still active. I had Phil Gleason come and stay with me at the White House. He has always been a good friend of mine. I have a great big history here in two volumes written by Charlie Hazen. He's made quite a name for himself writing history. Harry Field, you know, never married. Tried to tell me the last time I saw him how lonely he was, but didn't get a bit of sympathy. Could have married a dozen times if he had wanted to. Seemed as if he was always over-cautious. Our big man, President Seelye, is still with us. Northampton would not be the same place without him. Bert Connor has put up a three-story building right across from the Draper Hotel. Got his own office in it on the third floor. Dick Rahar has quit serving meals in the inn since prohibition. I always thought a lot of Dick."

And so he went on, conjuring up old jokes, recalling people that I remembered only vaguely through the mists of twenty years. He made only one reference to his change of state and that an indirect one:

"I'd like to have your two little boys come to the White House and see the animals. We've got a bunch of young rabbits that might interest them. Kind people send us animals, puppies, kittens, queer animals sometimes—wombats and such."

I carried away an impression of boyishness and light-heartedness which I had not associated with Mr. Coolidge in his more youthful days. The years had dealt kindly with him, his face was fuller. His personality had taken on a glow, a touch of eagerness. He had mellowed with the years. . . .

A recently published biography of several hundred pages winds up with the conclusion that to many who have tried to study Mr. Coolidge he remains quite unsolved. Those who seek a solution don't go back far enough. Calvin Coolidge is considered no enigma in Plymouth, Vermont. Nothing in the youthful Coolidge to excite the imagination of any New Englander born before the *Maine* was blown up in Havana harbor. In his early surroundings he was a perfect and exact type of what everybody was familiar with. No nineday wonder or puzzle to anybody. One recalls the story of the Down East Yankee who paid good money to see "The Old Homestead" back in the days when Denman Thompson played the part of Josh Whitcomb. The patron of dramtic art felt that he had been defrauded.

"Them folks on the stage," he complained sourly, "wan't no highclass play actors. They were just like our folks to hum."

In this narrative we have gone back twenty or twenty-five years in an effort to explain Mr. Coolidge. We could profitably have gone back 200 years. Mr. Coolidge is eighteenth century, frugal, simple, hard-bitten, set down in the twentieth-century age of jazz, extravagance in speech, dress, mad desire for pleasure, for spending. The age of mobility—light, heat, and power distributed in an instant over copper wires, intelligence flashed across continents, under oceans and through the air in the twinkling of an eye; myriads of flivvers darting to and fro on our public highways, a world on wheels, restless, avid, resistlessly pushing and struggling onward; fortunes made or lost in a day, big fees, high stakes. The riddle, the mystery, is not in Mr. Coolidge himself, but in the sheer inability to measure the eighteenth century in terms of twentieth-century standards.

He is a throwback to the eighteenth century. He is frugal along with his fellow mortals of the same epoch. They had to be frugal. Those sterile Vermont hills denied life to people who were not frugal. Mr. Coolidge does not know how to play. No more did his forebears. Life was too serious a thing. There was no time to play. The wilderness had to be subdued. A man went to church with a rifle tucked under one arm and the Bible under the other. The beauty of the external world never appealed to these men; their minds were taken up with the beauty of holiness. To them music and art were as sunlight to the blind. In the hard struggle for existence their æsthetic instinct had never been developed. It takes leisure to cultivate the muses. These men, too, were sparing in speech. Hardbitten of fate, their lives were a protest against extravagance in speech, in dress, in money expenditure. Mr. Coolidge is exactly like his forebears and doesn't try to be anything different.

Colonel Coolidge, the father, fell to talking of his son:

"My boy was always shy and quietlike and never put himself forward. It riles Calvin to have people show off. He was a trusty kind of a boy. Whatever I left for him to do, I never had to ask him later if he had done it. I thought when he was a boy he had the makings of a good doctor, but he told me he did not care for doctoring particularly; all he wanted was a good education. He always attended to whatever he had in hand and I guess he is attending right now to what he has to do.

"The other day I was looking over some old papers in the attic and found Cal's cash accounts in college. Everything balanced up— $2.50 a week for board, so many cents for newspapers and a bag of peanuts. Every cent accounted for. He never ran over his receipts."

Now surely these qualities are not unintelligible to Americans who know anything about the history of their country. Men of the Coolidge quality are the men who in its bleak, precarious beginnings made this nation. They were the hardy souls who, whether living in Virginia or Massachusetts, streamed westward, blazing trails, subduing the forest, fighting savages, conquering the wilderness. While England's ways have been the waterways of the world and the symbol of her greatness an ocean ship, our ways have been the blazed trails of a continent—the symbol of our rise to greatness the covered wagon.

We live in an extravagant, money-spending, pampered, high-powered age; but democracy has an instinct for self-preservation and that instinct makes democracy workable. The life of this nation is a bigger thing than a formula. Our nominating conventions, our scheme of cabinet government are quite unknown to our written Constitution. Our vigorous national life displays itself in constant adaptation to the changing conditions of an ever-changing world. In our restless, complex, high-keyed Western civilization we have not forgotten the slow grim men of our early half-starved beginnings in the wilderness of the New World. Through the self-preservative instinct, flashiality turns for help to durability. Our democracy is always finding an antidote to its own toxins.

Further, Mr. Coolidge answers to the demand for emotional relief, the necessity for emotional reversal. The revivalist and the actor understand the psychology of emotional reliefs. The revivalist keys his audience up to a high pitch of emotion, to the point where men and women begin to weep. Sensing the need for comic relief, he will tell a funny story and set everyone laughing. The expert vaudeville manager sees to it that sob stuff follows on the heels of the custard-pie turn, and vice versa.

The President's strength, I think, lies in the fact that to the great mass of the American people he is intelligible rather than enigmatical. He is not below them nor yet too high above them. He is not impatient with mediocrity and is understood by mediocrity. He has risen step by step in the public service just as a lad starting as a water boy for a railroad section gang works up through the entire executive hierarchy and becomes president of the road.

There's nothing new in all this to American experience. It is nothing new for our modern men to keep faith with the homely virtues of their ancestors. The roots of our great democracy strike deep into the soil of our Western world with its abounding resources and fresh opportunities. The topmost shoots like the myriads of lesser buds are fed from the same sap. There are tens of thousands of young men in this country not different in the essentials of character from the Calvin Coolidge of the Vermont hills; young men who with no hope of great achievement are content to do humbly their duty.

An Early Evaluation

By FRANK W. STEARNS

In 1935, two years after Calvin Coolidge's death, Mrs. Coolidge wrote of her husband's friendship with the Boston merchant Frank W. Stearns: "The acquaintance between Mr. Coolidge and Mr. Stearns which ripened into abiding friendship began when Mr. Coolidge was President of the Massachusetts State Senate. . . . Mr. Stearns knew and understood the President as no other man knew and understood him." The addressee of this letter, Robert W. Maynard of Boston, was a business associate of Mr. Stearns' and later became head of the firm, the R. H. Stearns Company.

August 16th, 1916.

My dear Maynard:

Having in mind our conversation of this morning about the two classes of people, small in numbers but very important, who, while they certainly support Coolidge for Governor or for any other high office, still question him a little—some because they think he lacks finish and might on some occasion of ceremony not fulfil all the requirements, and some because they think he is for Coolidge first, last, and all the time—I would like to express, if I can, my opinion of Coolidge.

You know our relations have been very intimate for the past two years. Why I first became interested in him about three years ago I do not exactly know. On my first knowledge of him, he offended me deeply, so I started without any prejudice in his favor. But in some way my attention was attracted to him, and I have come to feel very sure of certain things with regard to him.

First, humanly speaking, I believe that he is splendidly honest. For a young man he has been placed in a good many trying positions where if there was a yellow streak in him it would almost certainly come out. He has great courage. He told me once that when he first went into the Legislature he supposes he was considered a radical, especially along the lines of legislation in favor of social betterment. There came a time about the middle of his legislative experience when he came to the conviction *not* that his previous ideas were wrong but that Massachusetts, at any rate, was going too fast. As he put it, legislation was outstripping the ability to administer. He felt that unless we were willing to get into serious trouble that would take years to rectify, a halt must be called; and he faced about and was probably then considered a conservative. He said he supposed at the time that his career in public life was ended; that neither radicals nor conservatives would understand him. Apparently he did not realize what confidence people have in him. . . .

Many times during the last campaign, when I was chairman of Coolidge's committee, questions would arise which were entirely new to me. Several times when I asked him whether I should do thus and so he would tell me, "That is not fair to the other side," or "That is not entirely straight." And once he added, in answer to a question, "You know politics does not differ especially from anything else. In politics nothing is worth having unless you can have it in the right way."

For some considerable time I wondered whether his disinclination to talk was a pose. Since I have become well acquainted with his father and have listened to accounts of his grandfather, I have become convinced that it is an inherited difficulty, if you call it a difficulty. His father, who lives in a little town in Vermont of less than six hundred inhabitants, has a wonderful reputation all over that part of Vermont for just the qualities that are so strongly developed and so trustworthy in Calvin Coolidge.

Ex-Governor Stickney of Vermont, himself a man of high character, I judge, told me that the confidence and reliance that people placed in Colonel Coolidge, the father, is wonderful. He said that he as a young man knew the grandfather and he thought that beyond any man of his acquaintance he admired Calvin Coolidge's grandfather for his sterling qualities and for his almost uncanny horse sense.

As to Coolidge's appearance in public on some great occasion, I do not know that anything can be said. He certainly would never do anything foolish. He would give the impression to the audience that he gave to the foremen and superintendents and workers in George E. Keith & Co.'s factories. The verdict there, I believe, was that even if he would not talk, they realized that there was a man of sterling qualities that they trusted and would be glad to follow. He has, of course, none of the graces of oratory. There has been some discussion as to whether it was wise to try to make him give a little attention to such matters. Personally, I do not feel that it would be wise. He has a carefully thought-out method in all his work. It is his own. It comes to him from a long line of ancestry, and I think we should run great risk if we tried to change it. I used to be very nervous in the early days of the campaign as I went about and heard him speak on the same platform with one or two spell-binders—really fine speakers—fearing that strangers would not appreciate my candidate. I got bravely over it. I would sometimes sit toward the back of the hall in the midst of an audience, and I found that they were straining every nerve to catch just what he had to say and did carry away the point which he wanted to make, and the point had real value. As a writer he has few equals. His speech made when first elected President of the Senate was shown by a classmate of his to Theodore N. Vail, one of the great men of the country. Mr. Vail read the speech four or five times, and when he handed it back he said, "That is the greatest speech ever made by an American." When you read the speech and realize the courage that it took to make it, the clarity and force of the style, and the fact that the man's whole history shows that he would fight for his views, you will realize that while Mr. Vail may have exaggerated, there was a good deal of truth in his statement.

If it is important that we should have a Governor who can make as felicitous a speech as John D. Long could make on some occasion of ceremony, I cannot answer those who offer this criticism of Coolidge, but they should not forget that this is the *only* criticism to which Coolidge is justly open. He would make a fine appearance in any assembly, and after the people had gone away they would find themselves thinking over what he had said.

With regard to the other criticism—that he is for Coolidge first, last, and all the time—whether or not that is a criticism depends a good deal on just what is meant. If it means that he would treat those who differed with him or who were running against him unfairly for his own personal gain, I do not believe it. In the last campaign I heard almost every speech he made except a few in the extreme western part of the state. I cannot recollect an occasion in the primary campaign when he ever made any reference whatever to the other candidate or offered any criticism of him. Even when someone attacked himself, the audiences would never know from anything that Coolidge said that there was another candidate. His speeches were all addressed to the troubles that have crept into legislation and administration in Massachusetts and to suggestions of the remedy. If it means that he is not considerate and helpful to others, I know that that charge is not true. His methods are methods of action, not words, and he has fastened to him the best people in all classes of the community because of what he has accomplished.

I had an interesting illustration of this. A gentleman, the head of a large shipping firm, had occasion to go before the Council on the question of appointment of a pilot in Plymouth Harbor. An appointment had been made of a very young man who knew the channel well enough to bring in a fishing boat safely but had never been aboard a large steamer such as brings in valuable cargoes of hemp and sisal. The Plymouth Cordage people were very nervous about the matter. I happened to be just outside the council chamber when this gentleman came out, and I said to him: "Was Coolidge in there?" He said: "There was a man there who looked something like his picture, who said nothing and apparently did not pay much attention." A week later my friend called me on the telephone and said:

"That man Coolidge of yours is a star. I thought he was paying no attention. As a matter of fact, he immediately wrote to Plymouth to learn conditions in Plymouth Harbor, went personally down to the wharfs in Boston, made the acquaintance of some of the best pilots, learned what the real duties of a pilot are, and now has a workable plan for rectifying the troubles at Plymouth." This method of working is very characteristic.

Coolidge has ambitions. If the criticism means that he should not have, I should not be inclined to give any weight to it. I would not give much for a man who has not ambitions. If his ambition does not lead him into unfair treatment of his associates and opponents and does not lead him into doing something that is wrong, I doubt whether we can get very far in trying to weigh motives.

Anyone who is going to listen to what I have to say will probably want to weigh *my* motives for being so active in the support of Mr. Coolidge. I admit the motive of friendship, but I believe that my chief motive is a desire to see Massachusetts affairs in competent, honest, and courageous hands. . . .

Perhaps the best summary of Coolidge's character as I read it is, that among the clever orators, eager reformers, and shrewd politicians by whom he is surrounded, he seems to me to be the one man whose thought and work is all *constructive*. That is what I, in common with many others, have been looking for; that is what I believe I have found in Coolidge. . . .

F. W. Stearns

Calvin Coolidge, Politician

By KENNETH ROBERTS

Later to achieve fame as an historical novelist, Kenneth Roberts was, when this estimate was published in 1924, serving as a staff correspondent with *The Saturday Evening Post*.

CALVIN COOLIDGE is that peculiar and practically unknown paradox, a very good politician who is a very bad politician. He usually refuses to do, politically, what the politicians think that he ought to do, and he seems wholly lacking in the ability or the ambition to trade handshakes for votes.

He seems to be interested only in the right or wrong of big issues; and he never feels the necessity of making a decision because of the political effect that it will have on some political division of the country, which is extremely distressing to the old-line politicians.

The Coolidge political machine to all intents and purposes has always been a one-man machine, and the one man has been Coolidge.

Politicians from far and near came and breathed their time-tried counsels in his ear and twisted their perfectos nervously in their mouths, whereupon Coolidge applied another match to the charred end of his cigar, nodded thoughtfully and proceeded to do as he pleased—and the thing that he did was usually something that didn't please the politicians. Then the politicians would scream with horror, jump up and down with excitement and tell one another that everything was lost, after which Coolidge would carry the primaries in another state.

Or they would insist that something be done immediately if the President didn't want to lose the confidence of the country. He would hear them with all the impassivity of his Indian forebears, and wouldn't do it.

The politicians would toss up their hands weakly, and declare that they were through: that nothing could be done with that piece of Vermont limestone; that everyone might as well quit. And in a week or two weeks or so, the President would suddenly do the thing that the politicians said there was no use in doing so late.

Immediately everyone would spring to his feet with a shrill cheer and compliment the President for doing the thing at the exact psychological moment, and telegrams of congratulation would pour in from every part of the country.

Everyone who has anything to do with him agrees that he has an uncanny gift for knowing the exact moment at which to do or say the proper thing; but not one of the genuine blown-in-the-bottle politicians ever stops trying to make him do things when they want him to do them, instead of letting him do them in his own way.

Coolidge hasn't even a decent Kitchen Cabinet, unless someone with an inflamed imagination cares to regard Frank Stearns as a kitchen cabinet, which he is not; and this, from a political standpoint, connotes a terrible state of affairs. It's a terrible thing—for politicians—when a President uses his own judgment instead of letting the gang in on the good things.

He is not at all popular with the old-line politicians, and hasn't been popular for some time. So far as they have been concerned, he hasn't been on the cards, as the saying goes. No particular secret has ever been made of the fact that the politicians intended to place him neatly on the greased skids, if he had remained in the Vice-Presidential chair, and slide him rapidly and quietly out of the picture at the Republican National Convention of 1924. Naturally the politicians can't quite reconcile themselves to seeing him occupy the entire foreground of the picture. Occasionally they think it's all an unpleasant dream from which they will shortly awake.

There is consequently some reason to believe that Mr. Coolidge's campaign for the Presidency will be conducted along somewhat unexpected lines, and with a dearth of the old familiar political faces peering over the edge of the band wagon.

If he runs true to form, he will repair to the quiet upper reaches of the White House and ponder deeply over the exact meaning of such occurrences as, let us say, the Nebraska primary election, where more voters cast their ballots for him than they did for their own favorite son. He will interpret out of his own inner consciousness the meaning of those votes, and the things that the voters want him to do, even though their desires may be only partly formulated in their own minds; and he will have but little converse with politicians who seek to assist him in the interpreting.

If past history counts for anything, Coolidge's interpretation will probably be correct; and the interpretations of the old-line politicians would probably be incorrect. The old-line politician interprets according to his ideas of what he ought to let the people have, whereas Coolidge interprets according to his idea of what the people should rightly have.

As for the old-line politician who rushes to the front filled with a passionate and overwhelming desire to write into the Republican platform the customary rousing but moth-eaten cheers for the American eagle and the Old Flag, he is fairly certain to be handed his hat and asked, in the frosty nasal twang common to Plymouth, Vermont, and its purlieus, what's his hurry. . . .

There are, in Washington, large numbers of potential Presidential candidates and persons in high positions who maintain expensive publicity agents to send out tons of press notices and laudatory articles whenever their employers rid themselves of a few well-chosen words on any subject ranging from the effect of string beans on the growth of children to the damning effect of a bootlegger's testimony on the future of a great political party.

If other people want to do such things, Coolidge hasn't the slightest objection; but he has never had any desire to do them himself, just as he seems to have had little desire to do the conventional political things in the conventional political ways. He knows that he does a lot of things every day that have good publicity value; but he makes no effort to get publicity on them—a fact which causes great anguish to his political friends. His attitude is that whatever publicity he receives is purely voluntary, that such publicity is pretty substantial and very difficult to break down, and that it has an enduring quality that can't possibly be achieved by the reams and bales of publicity that are sent out by the more enterprising advertisers.

He will be forced by circumstances to use publicity representatives during his campaign for the Presidency; but there will be violent and hair-raising brain storms among the publicity men and the political friends, for he is going to keep right on doing as he pleases in his old familiar way. One of his high-minded publicity experts, for example, is going to come rushing into the President's office all aglow with some wonderful idea for publicity and place it proudly before the President; whereupon the President is going to stare at his desk with the pale and peaked look that is peculiar to him and say, in his best Plymouth, Vermont, manner: "No. Don't want an'thing to do with it." He won't bother to explain or elaborate on his decision, and the high-minded young publicity man will be very apt to walk right out past Pat McKenna and blow up with a loud annual report. . . .

There is always great grief in the vicinity of Coolidge when his friends and well-wishers begin to froth at the mouth over attacks that are frequently made on him, and urge him to train the Presidential guns on his attackers and blow them out of the water. Here the President's friends find themselves caught up a blind alley, for he has the feeling that his attackers are following an old established political custom, and that they have a right to this custom. He has never cared to use this weapon himself; and attacks of this nature cause him little irritation because of his feeling that the position of President of the United States is above such attacks.

If, however, some over-enthusiastic Congressman, let us say, should deliver an attack that would be an attack on the rights of the Chief Executive under the Constitution instead of a personal kick at Calvin Coolidge, it would probably prove to be a bird of another feather—of several other feathers, in fact—and the President would be quite likely to take his pen in hand and knock about six non-refillable holes in his attacker before he knew what had hit him. . . .

Many Presidents have been what is known as "reachable" in many matters; that is to say, they have had intimates and trusted assistants whose recommendations were frequently asked and frequently taken. Coolidge is wholly unreachable; and one of the few things that irritate him is the attempt on anyone's part to use the influence of someone who has access to him in order to get him to do some particular thing.

Such an attempt, he feels, shows that somebody evidently considers him incapable of reacting properly to the facts. Having proved through long public service that he can be depended on to react honestly and correctly to facts, he is most unpleasantly affected by any intimation to the contrary. His disgust may only be shown by a slightly elevated eyebrow or by a slight lowering of the corners of his mouth, but it will nevertheless be enthusiastic and sincere.

One of his most important acts while he was Governor of Massachusetts was the reorganization of the departments of the state, their reduction in number from something like one hundred eighteen to twenty, and the appointment of seventy new state officials. In this reorganization the Coolidge ax knew no friend; and he has said that it took more courage than the settling of the police strike. He had seventy appointments to make; and after conferring and consulting day and night as to whom the seventy should be, he locked himself in his office alone for about ten days in order to think the matter out.

His nearest friend had done some fluent guessing as to whom the seventy would be, and he was successful in guessing only three of them. None of the three was appointed to the position that the friend had guessed. Nobody "reached" him on any of the seventy. The only man who had a hand in the selecting of them was Calvin Coolidge; and his selections were of such quality that the Governor who succeeded him reappointed every man. . . .

Comparatively recent history will show that the position of next friend to the President of the United States is one that frequently brings dire misfortune in its train—such misfortunes, for example, as unexpected bludgeonings from the hand of the loved one, or offensive enlargement of the head, or delusions of grandeur.

Among the list of Presidential next friends, Frank Stearns so far appears to be the only one who has proved to be one hundred per cent efficient; and both the steadfast character of Mr. Coolidge and the old-fashioned honesty of Mr. Stearns—who, for example, has always refused to profane the Sabbath by advertising the wares of his large and excellent Boston business house in the Sunday newspapers of that city—are good indications that Mr. Stearns has a fair chance of leading the Presidential Next Friend League for many years to come.

During the early days of the Coolidge regime, the Washington correspondents regarded Mr. Stearns' frequent visits to the White House with the closest interest, and a number of them were inclined to accord him the proud position of fixer of the administration—the gentleman through whom Coolidge could be reached.

The only flaw in their reasoning lay in the fact that a good fixer, in order to preserve his reputation with the cognoscenti, should at least have an ambition for the role, even though he fails to deliver the goods; and Mr. Stearns, instead of blushing modestly at the insinuations of the correspondents, rudely refused the crown and even showed signs of decided peevishness—the first he had ever publicly shown—when various gentlemen approached him with propositions in which he was to play the role of king pin of the Coolidge administration. Stearns says openly that he wouldn't dare to attempt to influence the President.

Even the conductors of the Washington sight-seeing buses have given up their plan to advertise Frank Stearns as the power behind the throne because of the solemnity, sincerity, and convincingness with which he has set forth to everyone that his role, if he has one, is merely to attend luncheons and dinners which the President attends, and sit close enough to him to bridge over the Presidential silences with the social chit-chat and the airy nothings which are not a part of the President's cosmos, so to speak. . . .

The person who comes in close contact with Calvin Coolidge must be a singularly insensitive person if he does not feel sure of his sincerity, his honesty, his modesty, his reliability, his determination to do what is right.

And it seems reasonably apparent that for any person who dislikes or is suspicious of simplicity, stability of character, loyalty, thrift, sound judgment based entirely on the evidence, and a desire to alleviate ills with remedies that will cure instead of new-fangled and half-tried nostrums, Calvin Coolidge must always be a disappointing President.

The Genius of the Average

By GAMALIEL BRADFORD

Although he was also the author of volumes of fiction, poetry, and drama, Gamaliel Bradford's greatest accomplishment was in the realm of biography. His biographical style, for which he gained world-wide recognition, was unique in its methods of psychological analysis and appraisal, as exemplified in this study published in 1930.

IT IS AN interesting question how much of definite planning, of long ambition, went into the shaping and carrying out of this career. Coolidge's ardent admirers of course insist, as always, that he had no personal ambition, but was moved solely by the desire to do his duty and be useful. There are occasional contradictions to this view, but generally speaking even close observers do not seem to detect anything but an attentive and watchful consideration of whatever opportunity might throw in his way and a most zealous and industrious habit of profiting by it.

Nor is Coolidge himself any more ready to admit long ambition than are his admirers to admit it for him. The definite and repeated refusals to neglect any immediate duty for the sake of future advancement may of course be easily reconciled with ambition and may even be regarded as a farsighted and most politic manifestation of it. But constant references in talk, in his speeches, and in his autobiographical writing seem to indicate that Coolidge never looked forward very elaborately to a cloudy ultimate goal of his career, but took each step as it came, and was long inclined to bound his hopes with rather narrow possibilities, political, or even almost locally legal.

And when he had got to the top, how much did he enjoy it? There are signs, little indications and gleams, scattered everywhere, for those who know how to read, showing that he was well aware of the dignity and the grandeur and the far-reaching power of his office. There are shy and subtle touches, as in his speech to the Boy Scouts: "I am thrilled at the thought of my audience tonight, for I never address boys without thinking, among them may be a boy who will sit in the White House." Yet, along with the sense of greatness, there was always the sense of the burden and the responsibility: "It costs a great deal to be President."

The truth is, it was not in his temperament to enjoy glory or anything else. That temperament was the inherited, cumulative, aggravated temperament of New England, in which the sense of duty is the overriding force and an uneasy conscience always suggests that we are not in this world mainly to have a good time, or even to have a good time at all, but for some higher purpose. Always there is that New England face, with all its subtle implications, and the face seems peculiarly out of keeping with merrymaking or any of the riot of set publicity, most of all with the ludicrously inappropriate decorations which were resorted to in Coolidge's Western surroundings. There is the garish cowboy rig, and in the midst of it the chilly Vermont countenance, wondering painfully and wearily what it was all about. These people were not working: why should anybody want to do anything but work?

He never did, and here is the secret of his whole existence: work, unceasing, unresting, perpetual work, not so much for what was actually accomplished, but for the habit of work itself. In all the accounts of him this habit of work is emphasized, from boyhood up. . . .

So, when we dissect and analyze Coolidge's intellectual and spiritual life, we find the residuum to be simply an appalling, enthralling habit of work. The curious thing is that he does not seem really to enjoy even work. There are immense workers in whom the pure love of their occupation is so engrossing that it fills all their waking hours and makes every distraction seem dull and unprofitable merely by comparison. There is no suggestion of this state of mind in Coolidge. He works because he always worked, because his father and his grandfather worked before him and the instinct is in his blood; he works because he cannot help it. It recalls the remark which has recently been attributed to Miss Fannie Hurst in regard to her literary pursuits: "It is not that I am happy when I am writing, it is only that I am unhappy when I am not writing."

However this may be, it may safely be affirmed that the essence and the explanation of Calvin Coolidge is the rooted, dominating habit of unceasing, unquestioning, orderly, systematic labor.

The order and the system are just as marked in private life and domestic affairs as in public. The President kept a clean desk, but so did the Northampton lawyer, and the desk at home is just as clear. This is accomplished largely by an orderly and systematic arrangement of time. Every minute of White House time is naturally provided for, but here again the habit is constitutional and has always prevailed. . . .

Nothing shows the habits of order more effectively than Coolidge's dealings with money. It goes without saying that his temperament and his stern New England training gave him a caution and prudence in such matters which no opportunity and no abundance have ever shaken. It is not niggardliness or meanness. There is a perfect readiness to spend when there is a real object in spending. But the waste of pennies he could never get used to, never has. He has the only kind of thrift that really counts—the thrift that is an instinctive habit.

And it is hardly necessary to say that such an instinctive habit is of the utmost value to a great public official. It was carried into the practical administration of the national finances, and its value here is obvious and demonstrable, however judgments may sometimes have differed about the application. But the habit was even more valuable as an example to the American people in the huge orgy of regardless extravagance which the twentieth century in general initiated and which was so immensely augmented by the effects of the Great War. Here was a man who actually looked at a dollar before he threw it away, who actually hesitated to buy any luxury that was offered to him, merely because he did not know how he was going to pay for it. It was inconceivable, it was unbelievable. Yet this man had passed from nothing to the White House, and there might be good in his ideas after all.

Also, underneath the habitual thrift you must always recognize the strong, genuine vein of humanity in Coolidge which prompted his fine saying, "I am not trying to save money, I am trying to save people." The humanity seems to be always working, constantly, though covertly, in the money dealings as in other things. He was ready to pinch himself. He had no inclination to pinch others. In his law business he worked hard for his clients without much considering whether they could pay. When he was a legislator, his colleagues could get nothing out of him in words. They were often astonished to find that he had worked for their advantage when they were least aware of it. He kept up a quiet interest in the home people when he was away from them. One who had many letters from him says: "There isn't a letter in there that isn't packed with kindness, thoughtfulness, with messages to the home folks, and with numerous reminders of his strong affection for the people of these hills themselves. . . . Nobody could read these letters and think Calvin Coolidge a cold man." . . .

The interesting thing about Coolidge in his larger human relations is the strange combination of remoteness, aloofness, reserve, with such vast contact with men and women of all sorts, and even the apparent need of such contact.

As to the remoteness there can be no question: it hits you in the face everywhere. The man is by nature evasive, elusive, shy. In his boyhood he kept by himself, accepted others when he had to, but did not seek them. A well-known confession of his youth appears in a dozen more or less varying forms: "It's always hard for me to meet people. As a boy I would shrink with fear if I heard strange voices in the home, and would sneak up the back stairs rather than meet them—I simply can't get used to it." Thousands of New Englanders—and human beings—are made like that, but they do not usually work their way into the White House.

The evidence of others as to the reserve abundantly bears out Coolidge's own. "The fact is," said Judge Field, "that Calvin is shy. He dislikes the limelight. He hates to have his picture taken. He is an extraordinarily shy man and always was. The only thing that overcomes his shyness is his work." And the general spiritual attitude is summed up in the comment of one who knew him well: "He is the loneliest man upon earth."

The acme, the climax, of Coolidge's remoteness and reserve, of his asocial quality, is indisputably his utter disregard of conversation as mankind in general practices it. There are men who cannot talk even when they wish to. Coolidge can talk freely enough, but talk for talk's sake means nothing to him. If he wants to get information, he will pelt you, storm you, with a string of questions for half an hour on end. Then he has done with you, and you may go. The ordinary small talk of the world, its trivial gossip, drifts by him, slips over him, like the idle wind. He stands silent, apart, absorbed in his thoughts, and wonders how people can chatter so, and why they should.

The most extraordinary, the almost incredible, example of Coolidge's conversational habits is the story told by a competent witness of his sending for a friend, apparently for conference. Thinking he was wanted for his counsel, the friend hastened to answer the summons. He was ushered in from the waiting room. "How d'ye do?" said the President. "Sit down." The friend sat. The President sat—and looked out the window. After fifteen minutes of silence the friend rose to go. "Don't go. Sit down," said the President. After twenty minutes more of silence the friend rose to go. "Don't go; sit down," said the President. Another twenty minutes of silence.

The friend arose: "I guess you didn't want me for anything, so I'll be going." The President's reply was: "Thank you for coming. I wanted to think." Coolidge is sometimes described as an average man, and so in a sense he is. The average man might like to behave in this fashion, but he rarely does.

The element of humor may be taken as a minor aspect of Coolidge's conversational proclivities. Humor is sometimes denied him. And social laughter—laughter as a mere solvent, lubricant—he does not indulge in or require. But he has plenty of hard, dry, subtle wit, which may cause laughter in others, and innumerable instances of it are cited. Perhaps the best comment of all on the subject is Coolidge's plaintive remark, "Whenever I do indulge my sense of humor, it always gets me into trouble."

With these general social characteristics it is hardly to be expected that the loneliest man on earth should have many intimate friends. Evidently he has not, but those he has he clings to. The humble friends of his youth, like the Northampton cobbler, Lucey, remain his friends through everything. Perhaps it is better in the end not to have it said of you that you pick up endless acquaintances and throw them off when you have no more need of them, but rather that you "practically never lose a friend."

Another phase of the human relations is the question how far the influence of others has figured and made itself felt in Coolidge's life and character. Evidently some human contacts affected him profoundly, especially in early life. His father's influence and example went deep. The teaching of the Amherst professors, notably Garman in philosophy, on which Coolidge himself enlarges so much, took a solid and enduring hold. But of influence in the sense of effecting immediate result there seems to have been remarkably little, early or late. Coolidge listened to what everybody had to say, and then took his own course. Above all, no human being could ever boast that he was the President's accredited adviser or that a special line of action was suggested or initiated by him.

An equal curiosity attaches to the point of Coolidge's influence over others, doubly curious because it seems as if he were the last man who would have anything of the sort. There was never what is called magnetism about him, the enthralling personal hold of a Blaine or a Roosevelt. There was nothing of the cordial, back-slapping, drink-partaking politician, nothing whatever. Yet somehow he got the votes, somehow he got and held the confidence of the vast majority of the American people.

This was partly owing to his immense quiet observation of men, both individually and in masses. He saw everything and he remembered everything, at any rate everything that would serve his purpose. His judgment of men and their actions was not infallible, but it was keen, and it was always working. And on this judgment was founded an extraordinary political tact and skill. He knew what to say and do and just when to say it and do it. To be sure, he was cautious and deliberate in such action, and sometimes the extremity of caution exposed him to severe criticism, as with his apparent delay in the Police Strike, and again in getting rid of the dubious relics of the Harding Administration, and yet again as to the nomination in 1928. But even here good observers insist that the wisdom of his course was repeatedly justified by the event.

Finally, there is the question of how much Coolidge has really achieved politically. It must be admitted that he is not a great creative, constructive executive. He himself is said to have observed, in 1928, that it was now time for constructive statesmanship and that his own services had not been of this order and probably could not be. As I have indicated earlier, before the burden of direct governing had been laid upon him he showed a good deal of interest in progressive and for that day radical projects, and took hold of such things with the zeal and thoroughness that marked him in everything, so that he gained enduring credit with even labor leaders and radicals for fairness and honesty, as in the settlement of the Lawrence strike. But when he went into executive office he became more and more impressed with the immense importance of administration, and declared that it was imperative to give it a chance to catch up with legislation. And this idea seems to have possessed him more and more.

Is it not, after all, a wise and fruitful idea? Is not the failure in administration more than anything else responsible for the growing

distrust of democracy everywhere? A hundred years ago it was assumed that the ballot would make over the world. The world has
the ballot, and it needs making over more than ever. You have not
only got to have the ballot, you have got to have some means of
giving the will of the majority governmental effect—that is, you have
got to have efficient administration. It is precisely the lack of this
which has made parliamentarism a laughingstock everywhere. It
was the lack of efficient administration that brought Italy to the
benevolent despotism of Mussolini and Russia to the despotic benev-
olence of Lenin. In view of these things, perhaps, as time goes on, the
teachings and the methods of Calvin Coolidge may not prove so
futile after all.

There has been endless speculation as to the causes of Coolidge's
success. The astonishing contrast between the homely simplicity of
the man and the swiftness and smoothness of his political progress
makes such speculation inevitable. But his case is only a critical
instance of the puzzles that attend practical success and above all
political success in general. Why is it that again and again we see
brains, power, natural gifts, and even genius, apparently slighted,
disregarded, and pushed into a corner, while complacent mediocrity
makes its way to the top almost without effort? Sometimes it almost
seems as if leaders succeed quite as much by what they have not
as by what they have, and one may meditate long and deeply on Dr.
Johnson's remark that "men please more upon the whole by negative
qualities than by positive." The more one studies Coolidge, however, the more one comes to feel the truth of the excellent prize
editorial by Mr. Frank W. Buxton, on "Wh[o] Made Calvin Coolidge," to the effect that while many interesting persons and many
strange chances may have had a hand in Coolidge's advancement, the
main figure in that advancement was Calvin Coolidge himself.

Most of all what has made Calvin Coolidge is the fact that he is
an average man appealing to average men. The average man has the
votes, and if you win him the votes will come to you. Perhaps the
best way to win him is to make him feel that you are altogether
different, but assuredly the next best is to make him feel that you
are exactly the same. The common people early came to see in

Coolidge one of themselves. They saw a man with their traits, their habits, their interests, their social surroundings, and this man kept all these things unaltered in his steady progress from the bottom to the top. Observing this, the average man said: "Here is one just like me, who has made his way to the White House. It is immensely agreeable, flattering, encouraging; let us keep him there."

Moreover, as has been aptly suggested, the average American saw in Coolidge just the virtues that were supposed to constitute the American ideal and supposed to have made America. Coolidge incarnated thrift, self-denial, plain and simple living, straightforward, hard-headed honesty. The average American had heard that his fathers had these virtues and had made a great nation by means of them. He saw with a sigh that he had not much taste for them himself, and that his children had much less than he; but there was all the more reason why he should turn to a President who embodied them completely. . . .

Not the least interesting question that arises in connection with this long and complicated career is the question just how far Coolidge analyzes and understands himself. There may of course be depths of self-interrogation and self-study which are not apparent, but such depths are not indicated or even suggested in any written or reported words that have come under my eye. Certainly anyone who hopes to find them in the autobiography written at the instance of the popular magazines will be woefully disappointed, for a more unrevealing document has rarely been produced with any such pretension. Nine-tenths of it is a rehearsal of surface facts easily accessible elsewhere and the remainder, instead of being an honest search into the man's own character and motives, is merely an effort to portray such a boyhood and manhood as a future President ought to be expected to have. The whole story is in the main a compound of superficial, trivial narrative and the congealed sentimentality already suggested. Every word of it shows the deadly influence of the popular magazine, and the only question is whether the writer is trying desperately to write down to that level or whether the level is one that comes natural to him, either alternative being sufficiently unpleasant.

I find little evidence in Coolidge anywhere of an abstract general interest in the analysis of human motives. Now and then there is an interesting and suggestive touch, as in the remark in the autobiography, "In public life it is sometimes necessary in order to appear really natural to be actually artificial," or the still more striking comment on the political mind. But usually the emphasis is placed rather upon action than upon motive, and the undeniably acute judgment of men seems to be more a matter of instinct than of elaborate analysis: perhaps it is all the more practically valuable on that account.

So, it is not to be expected that one who does not analyze others should analyze himself, and such analysis seems to be conspicuously lacking in Coolidge. We have already seen his attitude toward his own ambition. If he has been actuated by long dreams and vast desires and purposes, he is not himself aware of it, or in such comment as he does make disclaims it industriously. There is no clear attempt to analyze his own abilities, or the nature or the working of them. There is an apparently genuine modesty in regard to them, and especially a naive astonishment that he could have got so far with any powers that he knows of: that is all. On the other hand, there is no particular consciousness of weakness or defect. I have referred to the admission of a lack of constructive statesmanship, but in regard to neither this nor any other insufficiency does there seem to be any marked appreciation of being inadequate to any office that may come to him. Fate or some higher power has put him in these places; it is the affair of the same higher power to see that he is equal to them. And a similar complacency shows in his curious, at any rate apparent, indifference to criticism. Every President is abused with a variety and virulence of savage attack which it would seem as if no sensitive spirit could endure, and even some very tough spirits have shriveled and withered under it. It appears to have little effect on Calvin Coolidge. He is doing his best, and no man can do more: why should he care?

In short, the sense of occasional failure, of discouragement, of disappointment, which inevitably comes with imaginative obsession by a high ideal, seems to be altogether absent from Coolidge's make-up. The highs and lows of life are taken as they come, without disturbance of sleep or digestion. There is not one trace or hint of that fascinating, inexplicable, haunting melancholy which makes the distinction of Abraham Lincoln, though Coolidge and Lincoln have been often compared. In one of the most striking passages of Renan's history he cuts down to the root of such melancholy: "A trait which characterizes great men of European stock," he says, "is that at moments they become followers of Epicurus; they are over-come with dissatisfaction and disgust when they are toiling with the utmost ardor, and after they have succeeded they doubt whether the cause they have labored for was worth so many sacrifices." There is nothing of this vague depression in Coolidge, nothing of such spiritual reaction and recoil. Instead, there is a persistent, insistent, certainly not buoyant, but aggressive and almost tediously reiterated optimism, which seems partly physical in its nature, and which always suggests a more or less conventional and traditional habit and attitude of mind.

We have already observed such a conventional attitude in Coolidge's political thinking. It is even more marked and obvious in his thinking on religious matters. And his preoccupation with such matters is everywhere prominent. Turn over his writings and speeches, and on page after page you will come across a religious allusion of some kind. America is under the special protection of a divine power. Democracy is divinely ordained for the salvation of mankind, and all the forces of the universe are working with it. Per-haps no passage better sums up the whole attitude than a paragraph from the Boy Scout address: "It is hard to see how a great man can be an atheist. . . . We need to feel that behind us is intelligence and love. Doubters do not achieve; skeptics do not contribute; cyn-ics do not create. Faith is the great motive power, and no man real-izes his full possibilities unless he has the deep conviction that life is eternally important, and that his work, well done, is a part of an unending plan."

It is impossible to question the absolute sincerity and profound conviction of this religious attitude. It is not only believed but lived, and no man ever carried his convictions into his life with more fervent and reverent piety than Calvin Coolidge. But the attitude is simply that of the Christian, not to say Fundamentalist, orthodoxy of the middle nineteenth century, or earlier. It is the unshaken belief in an anthropomorphic God, who guides the destinies of nations and also the petty affairs of individuals, and to whom it is of real importance what you or I or Calvin Coolidge may do or not do. Behind such a deity is a future, perhaps unending, existence, in which all the inequalities of this world, riches and poverty, brains and dullness, will be amply adjusted and compensated, and in which again, you, and I, and Calvin Coolidge will richly receive the reward of all our labor and endurance here.

Now this matter of religion, with Calvin Coolidge, is not a side issue. It is vital. On the theological fabric outlined above hangs the whole tissue and scheme of the Coolidge type of thinking and living —political, social, economic, and moral. If the theological fabric withers and collapses, what will you do then? Apparently for Coolidge it never has collapsed. But for millions of his fellow Americans there is very little of it left, and in consequence they demand a readjustment of the universe with which Calvin Coolidge can hardly provide them.

Who Made Calvin Coolidge?

By FRANK W. BUXTON

This editorial by Frank W. Buxton, Managing Editor of *The Boston Herald,* was published in September, 1923, shortly after Mr. Coolidge became President. For it Mr. Buxton was awarded a Pulitzer Prize the following spring.

WHO made Calvin Coolidge?
Margaret Foley, of course. When Levi H. Greenwood was President of the Massachusetts Senate he opposed woman suffrage.

She opposed his re-election in his district and prevailed. Senator Coolidge became President Coolidge on Beacon Hill, and the signals were set clear for the road to the Governorship.

Who made Calvin Coolidge?

Edwin U. Curtis, of course. When he was a sick man in that old brick building at the dead end of Pemberton Square, the heedless policemen went out on strike to the refrain of "Hail, hail, the gang's all here." The sick man showed the strength of the stalwart, until finally Governor Coolidge sent a telegram to Samuel Gompers that tapped his way into national prominence and is today a sort of magna charta of the people's rights.

Who made Calvin Coolidge?

James Lucey, the Northampton cobbler, of course. No explanation or argument is necessary here, but merely a reminder. The *Herald* published a facsimile a few days ago of President Coolidge's letter to him, which said: "If it were not for you, I should not be here."

Who made Calvin Coolidge?

Frank W. Stearns, of course. With as close an approximation to second sight as we may expect in these days, and with an ability to see around the corner years before Einstein told us how rays of light are bent, this substantial, self-made, self-respecting Boston merchant, with his quiet sense of an obligation which he owed to the community, discerned those qualities which hardly anybody else glimpsed. He left a Governor to go to the Republican convention and came back to pay his respects to a potential Vice-President.

Who made Calvin Coolidge?

Senator Crane, of course. He made him by showing him, in precept and practice, the way of wisdom and by vouching for him in high places where his chance say-so was as good as his oath and bond. He gave him that mixture of personal attachment and respect of which he was none too prodigal, but which was a mighty advantage to the few who had them.

Who made Calvin Coolidge?

The Republican party of Massachusetts, of course, a canny organization, with some Bourbonism, some democracy, some vision, some solid traditions, and no end of genuine appreciation of the merits of a trustworthy man. It always lined up behind him solidly, even when he displayed that reticence which to the unknowing was some evidence of ingratitude, and to the knowing was merely Coolidgeism.

Who made Calvin Coolidge?

The people of Massachusetts, of course. They took him at more than his own modest valuation, whether he wanted to be a town officer or a Governor. They had that which thousands call a blind faith in him, and which more thousands called a passionate intuition.

Who made Calvin Coolidge?

His mother, of course, who endowed him with her own attributes; his father, who taught him prudential ways with all the quiet vigor of the old Greeks who preached moderation in all things; his school and his college; his classmate, Dwight Morrow; his guest of a day or two ago at the White House, William F. Whiting.

Who made Calvin Coolidge?

Calvin Coolidge, of course! From the reflective shoemaker and the furious Miss Foley to the complacent Frank W. Stearns and the watchful and discerning Senator from Dalton, came some of the makings, but the man himself always had the essentials of greatness. Give another man those same foes and friends, and he might still be as far away from the White House as many another son of Vermont.

Puritanism de Luxe

By WALTER LIPPMANN

One of America's top journalists and a leading political analyst, Walter Lippmann was a member of the editorial staff of the New York *World* throughout Calvin Coolidge's years in the White House. The original form of this article appeared in 1926.

C. BASCOM SLEMP, who was once Secretary to the President, has recently published a book called *The Mind of the President*. Most of it is an anthology of Mr. Coolidge's utterances; but the first fifteen pages were written by Mr. Slemp. They are not exactly a blinding illumination. They contain the standard eulogy which is applied to all Presidents by their loudest admirers. For the President, no matter who he is, is always like Washington and like Lincoln in one or more respects, and it transpires that Mr. Coolidge is no exception to the rule. We learn that he is also like Andrew Jackson.

As a biographical device there are great, unexploited possibilities in this method. A man might write an analysis of Jack Dempsey in terms of Julius Caesar, Mark Antony, and Buddha. Paraphrasing Mr. Slemp he would say of Jack Dempsey that "in this respect his chief forerunner" was Julius Caesar who for a time was champion of the world. Adverting to Mr. Dempsey's private affairs he would say, "I think Jack Dempsey is like Mark Antony in this respect." In discussing the hero's disinclination to meet an opponent whom he might injure, the biographer would then compare him to Buddha who jumped into a fire in the guise of a rabbit to cook himself as a meal for a starving beggar, but first carefully shook off the fleas on his hide so as not to hurt them. Jack Dempsey could be described in this fashion, I insist, just as Mr. Coolidge can be described as combining certain of the better features of Washington, Lincoln, and Andrew Jackson.

But it is just as well to admit that in addition to the similarities there are striking differences. Washington, for example, was a rebel against constituted authority; he assisted at the creation of a government which had not existed before, and he presided over the government when it was necessary to make precedents instead of following them. Andrew Jackson led and consummated a social revolution; Lincoln fought and won a civil war. To compare Mr. Coolidge with these men is like saying that the contented captain of a houseboat on an inland river is in many respects like the captain of a ship at sea. Mr. Coolidge may be a great captain but he has never been to sea. . . .

Mr. Coolidge's genius for inactivity is developed to a very high point. It is far from being an indolent inactivity. It is a grim, determined, alert inactivity which keeps Mr. Coolidge occupied constantly. Nobody has ever worked harder at inactivity, with such force of character, with such unremitting attention to detail, with such conscientious devotion to the task. Inactivity is a political philosophy and a party program with Mr. Coolidge, and nobody should mistake his unflinching adherence to it for a soft and easy desire to let things slide. Mr. Coolidge's inactivity is not merely the absence of activity. It is on the contrary a steady application to the task of neutralizing and thwarting political activity wherever there are signs of life.

The White House is extremely sensitive to the first symptoms of any desire on the part of Congress or of the executive departments to do something, and the skill with which Mr. Coolidge can apply a wet blanket to an enthusiast is technically marvelous. There have been Presidents in our time who knew how to whip up popular enthusiasm. There has never been Mr. Coolidge's equal in the art of deflating interest. This mastery of what might be called the technique of antipropaganda is worthy of prolonged and profound study by students of public opinion. The naive statesmen of the pre-Coolidge era imagined that it was desirable to interest the people in their government, that public discussion was a good thing, that indignation at evil was useful. Mr. Coolidge is more sophisticated. He has discovered the value of diverting attention from the government, and with an exquisite subtlety that amounts to genius, he has used dullness and boredom as political devices.

I do not know whether Mr. Coolidge was born with this gift or whether he developed it by necessity in the absence of certain other political gifts. But I do know that in its present development it is no mean gift. The Democratic Party has good reason to know this, for the Democrats have been flabbergasted and routed by Mr. Coolidge's skill in destroying issues. The Democrats are simple folks used to heating themselves up to a terrific temperature over any issue. They only feel at peace with themselves when they are in an ecstatic broil. They simply do not know what to do with Mr. Coolidge. They hit his party an awful blow. They knocked three members out of his Cabinet and covered them with disgrace. And what happened? Did Mr. Coolidge defend his Cabinet? He did not. Did he denounce the grafters? He did not. Did he prosecute the grafters? Not very fiercely. He managed to get the public so bored that they could bear it no longer, and to make the Democrats thoroughly disliked for raising such a dull row. It was superb. To every yawp Mr. Coolidge can match a yawn. He has had the country yawning over the outcry against relieving the super-rich of taxes, yawning over Colonel Mitchell, yawning over the World Court, yawning over the coal strike. He has brought his technique to such perfection that one paper announced the conclusion of the coal strike in streamer headlines, saying "Coolidge Wins Coal Victory; Denies He Interfered."

This active inactivity suits the mood and certain of the needs of the country admirably. It suits all the business interests which want to be let alone. It suits everybody who is making money who wants to let well enough alone. And it suits all those who have become convinced that government in this country has become dangerously complicated and top-heavy, and that it is important to reduce and decentralize the Federal power. Mr. Coolidge, though a Republican, is no Hamiltonian Federalist. Mr. Slemp is right in saying that he has stopped, if not reversed, the Republican nationalizing tendency which runs from Hamilton to Roosevelt. He has just stopped it, mind you. He has not replaced it with anything. He has just stopped it while business is good.

The politicians in Washington do not like Mr. Coolidge very much, for they thrive on issues, and he destroys their business. But the people like him, not only because they like the present prosperity, and because at the moment they like political do-nothingism, but because they trust and like the plainness and nearness of Calvin Coolidge himself. This is one of the most interesting conjunctions of our age.

As a nation we have never spent so much money on luxury and pleasure as we are spending now. There has never in all history been such a widespread pursuit of expensive pleasure by a whole people. The American people can afford luxury and they are buying it furiously, largely on the installment plan. And in the White House they have installed a frugal little man who in his personal life is the very antithesis of the flamboyant ideal that everybody is frantically pursuing. They have not only installed him in the White House, but they trust him utterly as they hear his voice on expensive radio sets; they praise him as they ride in expensive motor cars; they toast him at banquets where there is more food than can be eaten. At a time when Puritanism as a way of life is at its lowest ebb among the people, the people are delighted with a Puritan as their national symbol.

They are delighted with the oil lamps in the farmhouse at Plymouth, and with fine old Colonel Coolidge and his chores and his antique grandeur. They haven't any of them the slightest intention of living in such a farmhouse if they can escape from it, or of doing the chores if they can buy a machine to do them, or of holding themselves aloof like Colonel Coolidge. But they are delighted that the President comes of such stock, and they even feel, I think, that they are stern, ascetic, and devoted to plain living because they vote for a man who is. The Coolidges are really virtuous people in the old American sense, and they have provided this generation, which is not virtuous in that sense, with an immense opportunity for vicarious virtue.

Thus we have attained a Puritanism de luxe in which it is possible to praise the classic virtues while continuing to enjoy all the modern conveniences.

A Darling of the Gods

By H. L. MENCKEN

H. L. Mencken, author, critic, and iconoclast, was editor of *The American Mercury* and a member of the staff of the Baltimore *Evening Sun* when he wrote this appraisal at the time of Mr. Coolidge's death in 1933.

THE EDITORIAL WRITERS who had the job of concocting mortuary tributes to the late Calvin Coolidge, LL.D., made heavy weather of it, and no wonder. Ordinarily, an American public man dies by inches, and there is thus plenty of time to think up beautiful nonsense about him. More often than not, indeed, he threatens to die three or four times before he actually does so, and each threat gives the elegists a chance to mellow and adorn their effusions. But Dr. Coolidge slipped out of life almost as quietly and as unexpectedly as he had originally slipped into public notice, and in consequence the brethren were caught napping and had to do their poetical embalming under desperate pressure. The common legend is that such pressure inflames and inspires a true journalist, and maketh him to sweat masterpieces, but it is not so in fact. Like any other literary man, he functions best when he is at leisure, and can turn from his tablets now and then to run down a quotation, to eat a plate of ham and eggs, or to look out of the window.

The general burden of the Coolidge memoirs was that the right hon. gentleman was a typical American, and some hinted that he was the most typical since Lincoln. As the English say, I find myself quite

55

unable to associate myself with that thesis. He was, in truth, almost as unlike the average of his countrymen as if he had been born green. The Americano is an expansive fellow, a backslapper, full of amiability; Coolidge was reserved and even muriatic. The Americano has a stupendous capacity for believing, and especially for believing in what is palpably not true; Coolidge was, in his fundamental metaphysics, a skeptic. The Americano dreams vast dreams, and is hagridden by a dæmon; Coolidge was not mount but rider, and his steed was a mechanical horse. The Americano, in his normal incarnation, challenges fate at every step and his whole life is a struggle; Coolidge took things as they came.

Some of the more romantic of the funeral bards tried to convert the farmhouse at Plymouth into a log cabin, but the attempt was as vain as their effort to make a Lincoln of good Cal. His early days, in fact, were anything but pinched. His father was a man of substance, and he was well fed and well schooled. He went to a good college, had the clothes to cut a figure there, and made useful friends. There is no record that he was brilliant, but he took his degree with a respectable mark, proceeded to the law. . . . Almost at once he got into politics, and by the time he was twenty-seven he was already on the public payroll. There he remained . . . for exactly thirty years, always moving up. . . . When he retired in the end, it was at his own motion, and with three or four hundred thousand dollars of tax money in his tight jeans.

In brief, a darling of the gods. No other American has ever been so fortunate, or even half so fortunate. His career first amazed observers, and then dazzled them. Well do I remember that hot Saturday in Chicago when he was nominated for the Vice-Presidency on the ticket with Harding. Half a dozen other statesmen had to commit political suicide in order to make way for him, but all of them stepped up docilely and bumped themselves off. The business completed, I left the press-stand and went to the crypt below to hunt a drink. There I found a group of colleagues listening to a Boston brother who knew Coolidge well, and had followed him from the start of his career.

To my astonishment I found that this gentleman was offering

to lay a bet that Harding, if elected, would be assassinated before he had served half his term. There were murmurs, and someone protested uneasily that such talk was injudicious, for A. Mitchell Palmer was still Attorney General and his spies were all about. But the speaker stuck to his wager.

"I am simply telling you," he roared, "what I *know*. I know Cal Coolidge inside and out. He is the luckiest goddam ＿＿＿ ＿＿＿ in the whole world."

It seemed plausible then, and it is certain now. No other President ever slipped into the White House so easily, and none other ever had a softer time of it while there. When, at Rapid City, S. D., on August 2, 1927, he loosed the occult words, "I do not choose to run in 1928," was it prescience or only luck? For one, I am inclined to put it down to luck. Surely there was no prescience in his utterances and manoeuvres otherwise. He showed not the slightest sign that he smelt black clouds ahead; on the contrary, he talked and lived only sunshine. There was a volcano boiling under him, but he did not know it, and was not singed. When it burst forth at last, it was the Wonder Boy who got its blast, and was fried, boiled, roasted and fricasseed. How Dr. Coolidge must have chuckled in his retirement, for he was not without humor of a sad, necrotic kind. He knew Hoover well, and could fathom the full depths of the joke.

In what manner he would have performed himself if the holy angels had shoved the Depression forward a couple of years—this we can only guess, and one man's hazard is as good as another's. My own is that he would have responded to bad times precisely as he responded to good ones—that is, by pulling down the blinds, stretching his legs upon his desk, and snoozing away the lazy afternoons. Here, indeed, was his one peculiar *Fach,* his one really notable talent. He slept more than any other President, whether by day or by night. Nero fiddled, but Coolidge only snored. When the crash came at last and the Wonder Boy began to smoke and bubble, good Cal was safe in Northampton, and still in the hay.

There is sound reason for believing that this great gift of his for self-induced narcolepsy was at the bottom of such modest popularity as he enjoyed. I mean, of course, popularity among the relatively enlightened. On lower levels he was revered simply because he was so plainly just folks—because what little he said was precisely what was heard in every garage and barbershop. He gave the plain people the kind of æsthetic pleasure known as recognition, and in horse-doctor's doses. But what got him customers higher up the scale of humanity was something else, and something quite different. It was the fact that he not only said little, and that little of harmless platitudes all compact, but did even less. The kind of government that he offered the country was government stripped to the buff. It was government that governed hardly at all. Thus the ideal of Jefferson was realized at last, and the Jeffersonians, who tend in these later days to be very well heeled, were delighted.

Well, there is surely something to say for that abstinence, and maybe a lot. I can find no relation of cause and effect between the Coolidge somnolence and the Coolidge prosperity, but it is nevertheless reasonable to argue that if the former had been less marked the latter might have blown up sooner. We suffer most, not when the White House is a peaceful dormitory, but when it is a jitney Mars Hill, with a tin-pot Paul bawling from the roof. Counting out Harding as a cipher only, Dr. Coolidge was preceded by one World Saver and followed by another. What enlightened American, having to choose between either of them and another Coolidge, would hesitate for an instant? There were no thrills while he reigned, but neither were there any headaches. He had no ideas, but he was not a nuisance.

The Thirtieth President

By HERBERT HOOVER

Prior to entering upon the Presidency himself in 1929, Herbert Hoover had served for more than seven years as Secretary of Commerce in the Harding and Coolidge administrations.

BEFORE Mr. Coolidge came to the Presidency, I had only a secondary acquaintance with him—such as one gets by dinner contacts. He was reputed to be a most taciturn man. This was true in his relations with the general run of people and with the press. With his associates there was little of taciturnity. Many times over the five years he sent for me to come to the White House after dinner just to talk an hour or two. He had a fund of New England stories and a fine, dry wit. After my election in 1928, he undertook to give me some fatherly advice as to how to run the White House. He said:

"You have to stand every day three or four hours of visitors. Nine-tenths of them want something they ought not to have. If you keep dead-still they will run down in three or four minutes. If you even cough or smile they will start up all over again."

Mr. Coolidge was well equipped by education, experience, and moral courage for the Presidency. He was the incarnation of New England horse sense and was endowed with certain Puritan rigidities that served the nation well. He possessed New England thrift to the ultimate degree, and his tight hold on government expenditures and his constant reduction of public debt were its fine expression.

He was most reluctant to take any action in advance of the actual explosion of trouble. One of his sayings was, "If you see ten troubles coming down the road, you can be sure that nine will run into the ditch before they reach you and you have to battle with only one of them." . . . The trouble with this philosophy was that when the tenth trouble reached him he was wholly unprepared, and it had by that time acquired such momentum that it spelled disaster. . . . The country was prosperous and I suspect that he enjoyed the phrase "Coolidge prosperity" more than any other tag which the newspapers and the public pinned on him.

Mr. Coolidge was a real conservative, probably the equal of Benjamin Harrison. . . . He was a fundamentalist in religion, in the economic and social order, and in fishing. On one of his summer vacations, when he started in that art to which he was a stranger, he fished with worms to the horror of all fly fishermen.

* * *

Mr. Coolidge was a man of complete intellectual honesty; and to him the worst epithet he could use about public men who privately professed one thing and who publicly advocated another, and who promised things they knew no man could bring about, was simply "demagogue." And he could amplify his diagnosis of such individuals with effectiveness. He was a man kindly and deep in his attachments; but he classed a quality in public men who engaged in backslapping and who at once addressed new acquaintances by their first names as a species of "infantile demagoguery."

Mr. Coolidge was without patience in face of corruption in public life. Here he became emphatic if not expansive. Upon a certain current scandalous transaction he remarked:

"Some people think they can escape purgatory. There are three purgatories to which people can be consigned: to be damned by one's fellows; to be damned by the courts; to be damned in the next world. I want these men to get all three—without probation."

* * *

Any summation of Mr. Coolidge's services to the country must conclude that America is a better place for his having lived in it.

A Wife Remembers

By GRACE COOLIDGE

A native Vermonter like Mr. Coolidge, Grace Anna Goodhue was born in Burlington, and, following her graduation from the University of Vermont, she began a course at the Clarke School in Northampton, Massachusetts, intending to prepare herself for teaching the deaf. It was in Northampton that she met Attorney Calvin Coolidge, and they were married in 1905; the bridegroom was thirty-three, the bride twenty-six. In his *Autobiography* Mr. Coolidge wrote, "For almost a quarter of a century she has borne with my infirmities, and I have rejoiced in her graces."

AS AN introduction to the personal reminiscences which follow, I shall recount an instance which occurred during the summer of 1905, about two months before our marriage.

Mr. Coolidge had come to Burlington for a few days' visit, and I asked him to go with me to the home of a college friend who lived eight miles out in the country. Rather reluctantly he consented, for it was never easy for him to make social calls. This was before the days of automobiles. There were perhaps one or two electric carriages in Burlington. Our only means of transportation was a horse and buggy from one of the local livery stables.

Mr. Coolidge made his preparations with extreme care. Wide silk shoe laces were coming into vogue, and he procured the widest, shiniest pair I ever saw, inserting them in his patent-leather oxford shoes with precision. He wore a dark-blue serge suit, new and perfectly tailored, and a black derby hat. At the last moment he placed a whisk broom in the back of the carriage. This is all so characteristic that I am recounting the story in detail.

Arriving at the home of my friend, Mr. Coolidge assisted me from the carriage at the doorstep, then drove the horse into the back yard and hitched him to a large ring in a corner of the barn. Every move was so deliberate that even now, as I tell it, the impression comes again, as it did then, of a small boy performing some hated task because his mother has asked him to do it as a favor to her. The hitch rope secured to his entire satisfaction, he took the whisk broom from the back of the buggy and brushed the dust and horsehairs from his clothing. Then, all spick-and-span, he rejoined me, and we entered the house. Introductions over, we seated ourselves, he on the very edge of a large sofa in the parlor. My friend was normally a talkative person, but our conversation upon this occasion was halting, and we received no assistance from the man on the sofa. Not one word did he utter and when, at last, he could bear it no longer, he arose and said simply, with one of his best smiles, "We'll be going now."

While he went to get the nag, my nonplused friend exclaimed, "My land, Grace, I'd be afraid of him!"

As we drove homeward I protested: "Now why did you act like that? She thinks that you are a perfect stick and said she'd be afraid of you."

Laconically came the reply, "She'll find I'm human."

I do not hesitate to say that I was a little "put out" at the time, but I have since come to understand. He realized that I was, in a way, putting him up for display, and he made every possible preparation to present an appearance which would do me honor. Beyond that his natural shyness would not permit him to go, and he would not make a pretense of enjoying the position in which I had placed him.

*   *   *

My mother and her son-in-law did not always see eye to eye. Both were accustomed to having their own way, which sometimes led to a test of authority.

The first instance of this occurred when the date of our marriage was under consideration. My mother maintained that I should resign from teaching and spend a year at home previous to the event. Mr. Coolidge took the position that we were both old enough to know our own minds, that he was able to support a wife, and that there was no reason for delay. In their conversations the wedding date was advanced until Mother took her stand at the following November, her son-in-law-to-be at October. Eventually he won in the draw, and poor Mother was bested.

I think she never wholly forgave him, but he proved himself so considerate and dependable that she had to admit that it might have been worse.

The wedding was a very quiet affair with not more than fifteen relatives and friends of the contracting parties gathered in the little parlor. The groom's father and stepmother, his Aunt Sarah Pollard and her husband, and Dr. McCormick, general manager for the groom, who "stood up" with us, were the only guests who came from out of town.

Dr. McCormick neglected to send a carriage for the minister who officiated. He was the Reverend Edward Hungerford, retired, and had been selected because at the time our church was without a pastor. A bare minute before the hour set for the ceremony he drove up to the house in much elegance behind his own spanking pair of horses.

Among our simple wedding gifts was one cherished above all others—a counterpane knitted by Mr. Coolidge's mother during the days of her long invalidism. This went with us in the bottom of my small steamer trunk on our wedding journey to Montreal.

We had planned to be away two weeks, but at the end of one we had seen everything there was to see, had attended all the theatres we could find, and I was not averse to falling in with Mr. Coolidge's suggestion that we cut our visit short. He made the amusing explanation that he was in a hurry to get back to Northampton in order to show off his prize. I knew better! It was his first political campaign which drew him. Perhaps it was a judgment on him that he lost the election, further mention of which will be made later.

While we were looking for a house in which to set up house-keeping, we lived for three weeks at the Norwood Hotel. It was about to close its doors, and has since been cut in two. The end in which our room was located was moved to the corner and converted into stores on the first floor, with living apartments above.

A large part of our domestic supplies was purchased from the stock of this hotel, so that for several years our sheets and pillowcases, our table linen and plated silverware, bore the mark "Norwood Hotel."

The process of my domestication was undertaken almost immediately after our return to Northampton. The first lesson was in hosiery darning. Sitting by a window one afternoon watching for my husband's return from the office, in accordance with the procedure commonly accepted as becoming a young bride, I saw him coming down the street carrying an odd little russet-colored bag. It must have been in the family for many years; it was antique in design and gave evidence of the wear and tear of time and usage.

Arrived indoors, my husband released all the little gadgets on the sides, and the bag revealed its contents. It was crammed full of men's hose, all in need of repair. I counted them—fifty-two pairs!

I was told that there were more where they came from. I applied myself to the task in hand. It kept me out of mischief for some time.

When I inquired if their wearer had married me to get his stockings darned, he replied quite seriously, "No, but I find it mighty handy."

*   *   *

. . . I wonder if [in later years] his thoughts did not return to the tough old pie which I set before him after my first attempt to produce an apple pie such as "Mother used to make." Our one maid had been taken ill, and I, inexperienced and ambitious, thought to surprise the family with my ability as a cook. Oh, that pie was tough!

We had not been able to make much impression on it at dinner. In the evening two friends of mine from Clarke School dropped in. My husband was unusually polite and attentive to them, and they were rather touched by his suggestion that I offer them a piece of my apple pie. He even went so far as to set places for them at the dining-room table. I am sure that the last thing they desired at that hour of the night was pie, but they could hardly decline so pressing an invitation.

Only those who have been placed in a similar position can imagine my feelings as I sat and watched them eat that dreadful pie, my husband also looking on with an inward glee of which I alone was aware. At last the final morsel was consumed amid loyal exclamations of approval. My husband interrupted to inquire in a serious voice, "Don't you think the road commissioner would be willing to pay my wife something for her recipe for pie crust?"

*   *   *

As a parent, Calvin Coolidge was a strict disciplinarian. He required and received prompt obedience. Yet he ruled by direction and precept rather than by force. It was seldom necessary for him to resort to punishment. Indeed, I can recall only one instance when it took the form of a good old-fashioned spanking administered with the back of a hairbrush.

His propensity for teasing was a natural trait which was handed down to him from his forebears. He could never get a great deal of satisfaction out of teasing Calvin, for his younger son entered into the spirit of it and enjoyed the encounter even more than his father did. But John was a more shy and sensitive child, and I could never get him to understand or adopt Calvin's method of outwitting his father. Occasionally John and I managed to turn the tables on his father, and we found that when he was the victim, the parent was even less amenable than the son.

*   *   *

Sometimes I wonder if Mr. Coolidge would have talked with me more freely if I had been of a more serious turn of mind. I do not think that he was very favorably impressed with my education. As a matter of fact, he definitely cast aspersions upon it when he asked me one evening, out of the blue, when Martin Luther was born. I had no more idea than the man in the moon, and I said so; whereupon he asked, "Didn't they teach you anything where you went to school?"

There were times, of course, when he talked, but it was more often about Plymouth and his boyhood than any other topic. We seldom discussed current events, history, government, philosophy or religion.

*   *   *

Mr. Coolidge's mind might be compared to a well-ordered household. Facts were stored away in orderly fashion where he might put his mental fingers upon them at an instant's notice. He read widely and with discrimination books selected with the object of "improving the mind," an expression which he used often. Occasionally he read a story published serially in a magazine, but seldom a book of fiction.

At the time of his marriage his library was contained in one small golden-oak bookcase of five shelves with a sateen curtain in front. Among the books were a set of Shakespeare's plays bound in red leather; a history of England in three volumes; several of Kipling's books, including *Barrack Room Ballads;* George Ade's *Fables in Slang; The Prince of India;* Longfellow's, Tennyson's, and Whittier's poems; a set of Hawthorne; the *Rubáiyát* of Omar Khayyám; Latin, Greek, French, Italian, and German grammars and lexicons; textbooks which he had used in school and college—about one hundred books all told.

He seldom added to this collection by purchase, but his library increased in size through gifts from friends and writers until it covered nearly every field of human thought and enterprise, numbering more than five thousand volumes. Mr. Harrison, in charge of the Forbes Library in Northampton, recalls that when we left the White House, about fifty-five large boxes of books were shipped to the library for temporary storage.

For many years Mr. Coolidge had little time for reading outside that which was required in preparing an address, but he was in the habit of reading after he had retired for the night. Books mounted in piles upon his bedside table, for he did not like to have them disturbed. Among them could always be found his Bible, the *Life and Letters of Charles E. Garman,* the Amherst professor whose influence upon his students was so marked, and *Paradise Lost* in two paper-covered volumes. These two small books he frequently carried with him when traveling.   *   *   *

If I were asked to describe New England people in one word, I should choose "thrifty." It is certain that Mr. Coolidge was a notable exponent of that quality, and he instilled it into his children. Calvin came by it naturally, but he disappointed his father once. We were on our way to Poland Springs, where the Governors of the New England states and their families were to be the guests of Governor

Baxter of Maine. He had included us in the party, although Mr. Coolidge was then Vice-President.

On the way we spent a night with Mr. and Mrs. Stearns in Swampscott. Mr. Coolidge overheard Mr. Stearns asking Calvin if he had received a present of five dollars which he had sent him as a birthday gift. Boylike, Calvin had neglected to acknowledge it. All the way to Poland Springs the following day, Mr. Coolidge questioned Calvin about what he had done with the money. After we arrived and had been shown to our rooms young Calvin was seated at the desk, given a pencil and paper, and bidden to write down all the things he could remember for which he had spent his five dollars. At dinner time he had not made much headway.

The following day was Sunday, an uncomfortably hot one. We attended service in the chapel. The visiting minister had a long sermon. There was no air stirring. I do not believe that many who were in the congregation followed the discourse closely. After we had left the church and were walking back to the hotel, my husband turned to me and asked, "Mammy, what was the sermon about?"

"Mercy," I said, "don't ask me!"

"John, what was the sermon about?"

"I don't know," was the answer.

Then it was Calvin's turn. The question was repeated. The boy squirmed uncomfortably, said he didn't know.

"Yes, you do, too," his father told him, and kept at it until, with a shrug of the shoulders, his son murmured, "Aw, spending money!"

＊　　＊　　＊

Economy . . . was one of Mr. Coolidge's watchwords. Moderation in all things governed his life. In no way was his economy related to stinginess. He spent in accordance with his means, but he watched expenditures carefully and was averse to waste of any sort.

Early in my acquaintance with him Mr. Coolidge expressed a desire to make a fourth at a picnic which the steward of Clarke School, in whose house he had a room, and one of the teachers and I were planning. After consultation with the others I told him that we had decided that he might join us if he would provide the lunch. To this he readily agreed. He brought two large chicken sandwiches for each, a shortcake split and buttered, with crushed and sweetened strawberries in a jar, and a dozen macaroons.

Having eaten heartily of the sandwiches and shortcake, we slowed down on the macaroons. After the meal, when our provider was picking up the dishes and the food remaining, he counted the macaroons and asked us in turn how many each had eaten. Half a macaroon was missing. For it no account has ever been made.

* * *

[Seeing a] reference to our wedding anniversary reminds me of another occasion when one was approaching. We were seated at the luncheon table with some friends. The President looked across the table at me and said, "Let's see, Mammy, when does our wedding anniversary come along?"

With the pretense of uncertainty, I removed my wedding ring and read the date, "October fourth."

Conceive my surprise when my interrogator declared, "That's all I want to hear about that."

I could not refrain from retorting, "Well, who is talking about it now?"

As a matter of fact I never reminded him of these occasions. Mr. Coolidge had deeper sentimental feeling than most people whom I have known, but he did not reveal it in outward manifestations. Indeed, I think that the only time he gave a present upon an anniversary, he handed it to me when I was crossing the lobby of the Touraine Hotel in Boston. My friend, Mrs. Stearns, and I were heading for the theatre. I thought it was some sort of joke, for the size and shape of the package indicated a toothbrush. Later, when I opened it, I found a flexible gold-and-platinum bracelet.

One Christmas in the White House his gift to me was five twenty-dollar gold pieces. Accompanying them was a card engraved with Mr. Stearns' name, bearing the words, "Compliments of the Season." I thought that I recognized it as the card which had come with a box of neckties from Mr. Stearns for Mr. Coolidge a day or two before. Later investigation proved that I was right.

* * *

Up to the time that he became President, Mr. Coolidge wrote his speeches on sheets of foolscap paper in pencil, going over them again and again, changing a word here, a word there, transposing and rewriting with infinite pains. When he had finished a speech, it was given to his secretary to be typewritten. None was ever wholly satisfactory to him at the time. Afterward he would read one and say, "That was a pretty good speech, after all."

When he became President, he began dictating his speeches to his stenographer, a quiet young man of inexhaustible patience, devoted to his chief.

Sometimes the young man would come to the President's study and spend a whole evening, his pencil poised above his pad, without making a single character. At last the President would say:

"That is all. You may come back at eight o'clock in the morning."

At other times composition flowed readily, and the stenographer would leave with his book well filled.

Among all the addresses which Mr. Coolidge made during his public life I know of only one which I suspect he did not write himself. It was delivered in Boston at a dinner given in connection with the celebration of the centennial anniversary of a well-known piano company. Mr. Coolidge was Governor of Massachusetts at the time.

Seated with Mr. and Mrs. Stearns in the balcony, I listened with growing amazement. The address dealt with composers and musical compositions in a way which indicated wide knowledge and discrimination in a field that lay wholly outside his study and experience.

When he joined us at the conclusion of the ceremony, I burst into laughter in which he quietly joined, a little shamefacedly, as I asked him where he obtained all that information. He did not commit himself.

Later, when Mr. Stearns . . . was arranging his addresses for publication in the volume entitled *Have Faith in Massachusetts*, Mr. Coolidge declined to permit the inclusion of the piano centenary address.

*   *   *

Up to the time that we went to Washington I had been a playmate of our boys, entering actively into their sports and amusements. I missed this association more than any other and sought for some form of activity through which it might be continued when they were with us on vacation. After the horses in the White House stables were at our command the boys became enthusiastic horseback riders. I had never ridden, but saw no reason why I should not attempt to learn.

At Fort Myer there was a competent Army instructor. I sought the advice of Mr. Davis, who was then Assistant Secretary of War, and he became my encouraging aider and abettor. After outfitting myself at a local haberdashery, I set forth in great secrecy one morning, accompanied by Mr. Davis, for the riding hall at Fort Myer to take my first lesson. Somehow the ever-vigilant reporters got wind of what was going on, with the result that there appeared an item at the top of the front page of the morning newspaper, bordered in black and headlined, "Mrs. Coolidge Takes Up Riding."

It had the semblance of a death notice. It certainly resulted in tolling a death knell to my hopes when the President, seated at the opposite side of the breakfast table, unfolded his paper and read of my latest venture.

With a look of surprise mingled with anxiety and disapproval, he dashed my adventurous spirit with, "I think you will find that you will get along at this job fully as well if you do not try anything new."

*   *   *

I knew nothing of the conducting of affairs in the Executive Offices or in the Executive Departments, considering that they lay outside my province. If I had manifested any particular interest, I feel sure that I should have been properly put in my place. At any rate I had my hands full discharging the duties of the position to which I had not been elected.

There had been times when I had protested against further advancement up the political ladder. My natural inclination was a little more domestically inclined. In spite of my protestations, Mr. Coolidge delighted in saying to those who seemed interested in my reactions to public life, "She has kept me running for public office ever since I married her."

II

WHITE HOUSE YEARS

Walking with the President

By EDMUND W. STARLING

From the first term of Woodrow Wilson to Franklin D. Roosevelt's third, Edmund W. Starling was a member of the Secret Service detail which is assigned to the White House for the protection of the Chief Executive and his family. Throughout the period 1923-29 he maintained a particularly close association with President Coolidge.

WHEN WE LEFT the cemetery at Marion [following President Harding's funeral], Jervis and I were, temporarily, free men. Our duty to President Harding had ended, our duty to President Coolidge had not begun. Other members of the [Secret Service] detail were watching him. On the ride back to Washington we relaxed, and when we arrived there I went to my room and slept the clock around. I was completely exhausted, and did not report for duty for another day. Then, at a quarter of six in the morning, I went to the Willard Hotel [where the Coolidges remained while Mrs. Harding prepared to move from the White House] and waited outside the President's suite on the third floor. I had heard that he was an early riser. At a quarter after six the door opened and he stepped out, dressed to go for a walk. He recognized me and said:

"Good morning, Colonel Starling, I've been wanting to see you. I want you to stay with me during my administration."

I had no hesitancy in answering him. He was a Congregationalist from the hills of Vermont; I was a Presbyterian from the hills of

Kentucky. Though between such people there is a multitude of differences, the basis of their character is alike. This small but well-built man with reddish hair, soft . . . eyes, and a determined chin, was easy for me to read in general outline. He was honest, brave, religious, and stubborn. With such a man I could get along.

"I will be most happy to remain with you," I said. "I will consider it an honor to serve you in any way."

Instead of answering he walked to the stairway. I followed him. We descended three flights of stairs and went out to F Street, walking toward the Washington Hotel. A few newspaper photographers, already versed in the new President's habits, were waiting. He posed for them; then we continued, following the lines of the Washington Hotel around to Pennsylvania Avenue, turning into E Street and walking east to Twelfth, where we crossed and stopped in front of the Martha Washington candy shop. Here the President spoke for the first time since greeting me. I had presumed he was busy with deep thoughts and had not bothered him.

"Do they make good candy here?" he said.

Before I could pull myself together and reply he answered himself: "They must. My wife likes it."

We did some more window-shopping, then walked back to the hotel. There was no further conversation. At the door of his suite I left him and went to get my breakfast. That afternoon we took another walk. Crossing Fourteenth and F Streets he yanked my coattail.

"Better be careful," he said. "That was a woman in a Ford, and that's a bad combination. One of them struck me in Northampton and bruised my hip."

Next morning we strolled again before breakfast, and I realized it was going to be habitual. At that time I was living at Thirteenth and Kenyon Streets, and in order to get to the Willard on time I found I would have to get up at four o'clock. While I was pondering what to do about such a predicament the President one day made a suggestion. We were in front of the Willard.

"You ought to move in here," he said. "It's a good place."

So I did, and remained there throughout his two terms of office, eventually getting a private telephone wire installed between my room and the White House. . . .

At the White House I waited outside each morning for President Coolidge, going into the lobby if the weather was bad. By a simple procedure, without saying a word, he showed that he had chosen me for his walking companion. When I was not on duty early in the morning he did not go out. . . .

I was distressed to find that he took no other exercise except walking. He did not play golf, ride horseback, fish, hunt, swim, bowl or even play billiards. He had no hobbies, not even stamp collecting. Moreover, he walked with his head thrust forward, his hands clasped behind him, his shoulders hunched, and his chest sagging. I finally got up enough courage to tell him that since he walked for a healthful purpose he should not defeat that purpose by his posture.

"It will do you so much more good," I said, "if you will keep your head up and your shoulders back, with your arms swinging. The important thing is to stimulate circulation in the chest."

He paid no attention to me, and for a week continued to walk as before. Then one day he suddenly struck out with his head stuck up in the air and his arms flailing, so that I had to walk at least three feet from him. I said nothing. After a while his arms fell into a normal swing. He never walked again with them behind him.

He liked to go to F Street and window-shop. To get there we passed the Treasury building. The walk in front of it at that time was in wretched condition. The flagstones had lost their uniformity of level and formed pockets which filled with rain whenever there was a shower.

One day I noticed a young lady whose stockings were wet half way to her knees with water splashed from these puddles. I called the President's attention to her and commented on the state of the pavement.

"Yes," he said, "the Treasury Department ought to fix it. If they don't, some day my Secretary, ol' Andy Mellon, will come walking along here counting his coupons and stub his toe."

Everybody was "ol' " to him. I was "ol' Colonel Starling," Frank

Stearns was "ol' man Stearns," Rudolph Forster [the executive clerk] was "ol' man Forster," and his Cabinet members were "ol' man Mellon," "ol' man Denby," etc. In the same way they were all "my": "my Secretary of the Treasury," "my Secretary of the Navy," "my Secret Service man." All the material trappings of the Presidency were likewise "my": "my car," "my house," "my lawn," "my garden," etc.

This feeling of ownership was a part of his attitude which puzzled me. He was not particularly proud of being President; he hated arrogance and conceit in all their forms. It was as if he were a small boy whose daydream of being king had suddenly been made real by the stroke of a magic wand. He would almost tiptoe around, touching things and half smiling to himself. In his high shoes and his great galluses he was an odd sight in the White House corridors.

On awakening in the morning he would walk across the upstairs hallway to the Lincoln room in his long nightgown and slippers. There he would peek out the window to see whether I was on the lawn. I stood there each morning taking my setting up exercises while waiting for him. If he did not see me he would have Brooks telephone downstairs to ask if I were in the building.

When he was satisfied that I was waiting he would dress and come downstairs. Sometimes he would tell the elevator operator to take him to the basement. Then he would try to sneak out the East or the West entrance, just to fool me. Everyone on the staff cooperated with me and tipped me off, so I was always able to catch him. . . .

His appetite for pranks was insatiable. In the afternoon we sometimes left for our walk from the Executive Offices. If the mood suited him he would press the buzzer which notified everyone that he was on his way to the White House. Then, while ushers, policemen, doormen, and elevator operators were rushing about getting things ready and snapping to attention, we would stroll out West Executive Avenue and leave them. . . .

The first time I heard him laugh was one afternoon as we set out for our walk. He was smoking a cigar, and as we approached the gate he took it from his mouth and flipped it to the lawn—he never smoked while walking outside the White House grounds. The cigar struck the ground in a shower of sparks just in front of a squirrel, who jumped straight up in the air. He turned before he hit the ground. In a moment he was up a tree and out on a limb, where he sat staring at us in surprise and disappointment. His look of disillusionment was almost human. The President laughed until he had to hold his sides.

The serious side of his job he performed so ably that the staff in the Executive Offices soon relaxed. Rudolph Forster was able to lead a normal life again. He had been busy all through the Harding years, for Harding had trouble with details and paper work, and Rudolph had to work overtime.

"The little fellow wades into it like Wilson," he said. "He knows what he is doing and what he wants to do. He doesn't do anyone else's work either. He'll be all right at this job. He does a lot of thinking, and he looks a long way ahead."

It was true that he didn't do anyone else's job. One day his personal secretary, Ted Clark, came to the office and asked if he could show the President a file of papers which Secretary of Labor Davis wanted him to read.

"He would like to know whether you agree with his decision," Clark said.

"I am not going to read them," the President said. "You tell ol' man Davis I hired him as Secretary of Labor and if he can't do the job I'll get a new Secretary of Labor."

One evening as we came home at dusk I noticed a light burning in the office of the Secretary of Navy, Mr. Denby. I remarked that Denby was a hard worker, frequently staying in his office until late at night.

"He must be an excellent man for the job," I said.

"I wouldn't say that," the President replied. "I don't work at night. If a man can't finish his job in the day time he's not smart."

A few months later the newspapers were proclaiming that the only thing of which Denby was guilty in connection with the oil scandals was stupidity.

His uncanny judgment of people, and the things he knew about them, always amazed me. Once I described a certain man as stingy, and the President immediately reeled off a list of important contributions to charity which the man had made, and added that he had just sent a young fellow to Colorado for his health and was taking care of his family, which consisted of a wife and four small children.

He was so different from President Wilson that it was hard to realize the two were fundamentally alike. For both of them life was largely a mental experience, but whereas in Wilson this was obvious, in Coolidge it was not. I could never figure out, as we walked along silently, whether his mind was busy with great affairs of state or trivialities. In the end I decided that most of the time he let his worries drop back to the subconscious and enjoyed himself like a small-town boy strolling down Main Street on Saturday night. The things he said to me might have been said in Northampton, Hopkinsville, or Lexington, Virginia. Passing a large department store one morning he said, "If you ever get married don't let your wife buy anything in there. My wife goes in there and it costs me a lot of money."

One afternoon we walked up Sixteenth Street to Scott Circle. Traffic was heavy and I had a difficult time piloting him safely across the street. As we continued west on Rhode Island Avenue he suddenly asked, "Who was the lady in the limousine wearing a red hat?"

"I didn't notice," I said, "but it might have been either Mrs. Alice Roosevelt Longworth, who lives on Massachusetts Avenue, or Mrs. Frank B. Kellogg, who lives up the way on Eighteenth Street. They both wear red hats."

We continued in silence, turning into Connecticut Avenue and walking south to the Mayflower Hotel, where we window-shopped one of the exclusive little stores.

"Think they're making any money?" he asked.

Nothing more was said until we reached the White House and he was in the elevator. Turning to bid me good-by, he said:

"Guess that was ol' lady Kellogg."

Mrs. Coolidge had occasion now and then to visit Northampton. Her mother was ill, and she herself found the climate of Washington difficult to bear. She was bothered with sinus trouble, and the Capital weather seemed to make it worse. One morning when she was away the President said to me as we returned from our walk, "Want to have supper with me?"

"I would be delighted," I said, wondering what time dinner would be served.

"Come on then," he said, walking into the elevator.

We went upstairs and into his bedroom, where he telephoned for two breakfasts. He didn't ask me what I wanted; he just told the cook to make his order double. It was served in the room, and consisted of fruit, oatmeal, bacon and eggs, coffee, toast and marmalade. Every morning thereafter when Mrs. Coolidge was away I shared this "supper" with him (every meal to him, I discovered, was "supper").

Whenever a letter was expected from Mrs. Coolidge we ended our walk at the Executive Offices, where he cut the twine on the stacks of his personal mail and looked through it until he found an envelope addressed in her handwriting. He would stuff it into his pocket and walk quickly to the White House. I would go up with him on the elevator but remain outside his room until he sent for me. He would lock the door, and it was often as much as half an hour before he opened it again and asked me in.

He loved his wife deeply. He was, of course, a very sentimental man, and a very shy one. He loved a few people a great deal, and he was embarrassed about showing it. Gradually, as time went by, I found him to be so human and thoughtful that I came to the conclusion his outward reticence and aloofness were part of a protective shell.

On summer nights when Mrs. Coolidge was away we sat on the back porch together and smoked and talked—he made me smoke his big, black cigars and they nearly knocked me out. Often then he spoke at length of his boyhood in Plymouth, of his deep affection for his mother, of her fair-haired beauty, of her love for flowers, of her understanding of him, and of the help she gave him in the problems he faced from day to day. He seemed to remember every day he had spent with her. She died when he was young, and he nourished his memories so that now they were living things, as real to him as the days he now was living. He communed with her, talked with her, and took every problem to her.

"I wish I could really speak to her," he said one night. "I wish that often."

He clung to the habits of his boyhood as well as the memories. When we returned from our afternoon walks he would take me to the butler's pantry and make two sandwiches of Vermont cheese, one for himself and one for me. He cut the cheese carefully, measured the sandwiches one against the other, and if they were not equal would shave off a little more cheese to make the balance. Then he would give one to me and we would sit down and eat them. The cheese was as strong as a billygoat. One day he said to me, "I'll bet no other President of the United States ever made cheese sandwiches for you."

"No," I said. "It is a great honor."

He added gloomily: "I have to furnish the cheese too."

He would go upstairs to his bedroom and eat crackers covered with preserves. He always kept a supply in his room. He ate nuts and peanuts too, and the peanuts were unparched. It was amazing that he never got fat.

One day as we passed the stand of the White House peanut vendor he sniffed at the roasting chestnuts, stopped, and put his hand into his pocket. It came out empty and he turned to me.

"Colonel," he said, "can you lend me ten?"

"Ten dollars?" I said, reaching for my wallet.

"No," he said, "ten cents."

I gave him a dime and he bought the chestnuts. Some time after our return to the White House the elevator operator brought me an envelope. Inside it was a dime.

Later I became his banker on our walks, furnishing him with dimes and nickels for peanuts, magazines, and newspapers. I kept an account of my advances in my notebook, and every once in a while he gave me fifty cents to clear up the debt. . . .

Not long after he entered the White House I saw evidence of his irascibility for the first time. He appeared one afternoon with a lock of sandy-colored hair showing from under his hat and the tip of his nose red. We walked rapidly toward Connecticut Avenue. At Jackson Place he said in a low, surly tone:

"I'm not going."

I didn't say anything. A few blocks later he said:

"I'm not going, and I'm not going to let that wife of mine go."

Some sort of comment was called for, I thought, so I said, "You certainly ought to follow your own judgment."

After a few more blocks he said:

"When I lived at the Willard and was Vice-President they didn't know I was in town. Now that I'm President they want to drag me up to their house for one of their suppers and show me off to a lot of people, and I'm not going."

I remembered the invitation now. It was from the current Washington social queen.

"I'm not going, and I'm not going to let that wife of mine go," he repeated.

He didn't, either.

In time I grew to expect anything of him, and he never failed me. One morning we were having "supper" in his room and I heard someone pacing up and down in front of the door. I was seated with my back to it and I looked nervously around several times as the pacing continued. The President noticed it.

"That's just ol' man Stearns," he said. "He wants to come in and have some of our supper, but I'm not going to let him. He's eaten enough of my food already this morning."

Stearns, I discovered, had a habit of rising early and eating breakfast by himself. He then smoked a cigar and took his exercise by walking up and down the corridor.

One Sunday morning about a year after I had moved into the Willard, I was half way through shaving at six-thirty when the telephone rang. It was the night clerk. He was greatly excited. President Coolidge, he said, had just walked into the lobby on the Pennsylvania Avenue side and wanted to know if I could come down immediately.

I washed the lather off my face, leaving half of it unshaved, put on my shirt, tucked my coat and vest under my arm, and ran for the steps, knotting my tie as I fled down the hallway. I went down the steps three at a time to the main floor level on the F Street side of the building. As soon as I hit bottom I began wriggling into my coat and vest, when a voice just over my shoulder said:

"I thought you'd come down this side."

He had walked through Peacock Alley to meet me, and was chuckling at his shrewdness in having correctly guessed which way I would descend.

While he watched I buttoned my vest and coat, straightened my tie, and set my hat straight on my head. Then we went out for our walk.

The President and His Mail

By IRA R. T. SMITH

Ira R. T. Smith, former Chief of Mails at the White House, joined the staff of the Executive Offices of the President in 1897 during the administration of William McKinley, and his service continued for a period of over half a century.

I USUALLY got to the office about 8 A.M. in order to have the mail in readiness when the staff arrived, and after the President had taken his morning walk. Along toward 8:30 I would usually see him coming back to the White House with one Secret Service man, probably Colonel Edmund W. Starling, walking beside him, and another following closely. . . .

When he turned into the White House grounds after his walk he would head straight for the basement driveway at a fairly fast clip. Then just as he came opposite our office door he would sometimes make a sharp right turn so unexpectedly that the momentum of the Secret Service men would carry them on to the driveway before they could stop, while the President would be entering the office alone and with a pleased expression on his face. He would walk into my office, look down his sharp nose at me, and say: "Good morning. Are there any mails for me?" Or he often asked particularly if there were "mails" from his father. I would have his personal letters ready and he would carry them off to his office. He had a thorough knowledge of the office, and would often go himself to the files for records.

On mornings when I was late to work I might find him sitting in my chair, with his feet on the desk, reading letters he had sorted out of the mail. On such occasions he would not even look at me, and instead of saying anything, I would go to another desk, sit down, and twiddle my thumbs until he decided to leave. He usually departed without speaking to me, and I felt that if I had offered any explanation of my failure to beat him to the office he would have merely sniffed and walked away.

I don't know whether the President ever sat with his feet on his own desk, but I was always glad he chose to park his shoes on mine on those occasions. I always enjoyed doing it myself, and if anybody raised an eyebrow at me I pointed out that what was good enough for Mr. Coolidge was good enough for me. I always felt that way about the Coolidge administration in general, too, because it was the most enjoyable of all from my viewpoint. Right now I feel that I never want to open another letter of any kind, but if I could work for Mr. Coolidge, I'd be happy to go back on the job tomorrow—provided both of us could get some time off for fishing.

Mr. Coolidge was a master of dry and dead-pan humor. He never smiled at his own jokes, and if you wanted his respect, you never acted more than moderately amused. He didn't face you when he was making a joke, but he always cut his eyes around to see whether you caught it. This put quite a strain on some members of the staff who either were inclined to laugh out loud, or who weren't always sure when it was a joke. I usually found his jokes of a caliber that enabled me to restrain my laughter, and we got along fine.

Once when an Ohio Congressman was making a big front-page

fuss about bureaucratic wastefulness and idleness, Mr. Coolidge came into the office and saw Charley Wagner, the chief stenographer, with his feet on a desk and a newspaper opened so that his face was covered and he failed to see the President. Mr. Coolidge walked up to him, tapped at the paper, and said severely, "That man from Ohio will get after you." Then he hurried away. Wagner never was sure whether he was being ribbed.

On another occasion the President came into the office and examined some packages that had just arrived. He was apparently about to open a big one when I reminded him that it was against Secret Service orders for the President to open any packages. He was a bit peevish about it, and since I knew what was in the package because of a letter received earlier, I told him I would open it while he watched. It turned out to be a big and costly picture frame that held a very gaudy and unattractive colored photograph of a locomotive, sent in with the compliments of the manufacturers. The President looked at it in petty disappointment, and then, cutting his eyes toward me, said:

"Well, send it over to the house. Mama can make good use of that frame.". . .

One day the President stopped at my desk and asked me whether his son John received much mail. John was a likable and good-looking kid, and he had been getting a good deal of fan mail, especially from teen-age girls who wanted the thrill of writing to a boy in the White House. Some of these letters from girls he didn't know were clever, and occasionally John would answer one of them with a flippant note.

I told Mr. Coolidge that there were usually some letters for John every day or so. He nodded, and said that hereafter I was to send them to him instead of the boy. The next day John wandered in, acting a bit too casual. We talked about nothing much until he finally asked whether his father had given me instructions about his mail. I told him what had happened.

"Well," he said, with some embarrassment, "it doesn't matter except for one thing. You see, there's one that's different. I don't mind Dad getting the others, but this one—you know the one I mean?"

Yes, I said, I believed I knew the one.

"You know she's an old friend, and not like the crazy ones that just write in without knowing me. I wondered if maybe—"

"John," I said, "I'm sorry, but I have very definite orders from the President and you'll have to work it out with him." The boy's face showed how he felt about *that*. So I went on:

"Of course you know how we do things here. I sort out your letters each morning and put them in a pile right there on the corner of my desk. Then I sort the other letters. Sometimes I even have to go out of the room for some reason or other. Then later I send the letters over to your father."

John gave me a long, pleased look and departed. The next morning I sorted out his letters, and there was one from *the* girl. I kept an eye on the door, and when I saw John coming I got up and went elsewhere. When I came back *the* letter was gone and so was John. We worked it that way for quite a while, and I don't think we ever missed a trick. I guess our little trick was all right, because later John married the girl. She was Florence Trumbull, daughter of the Governor of Connecticut.

The President was not a generous giver, but he always wanted to do the right thing. One day he walked up to my desk and suddenly handed me a box of cigars.

"Have some tobaccah," he said. Then he walked on down to the desk of Nelson Webster, the disbursing officer, and repeated the performance. Webster and I later compared notes and found that he had taken the trouble to discover what price cigars each of us smoked. Webster smoked twenty-five-centers and he got twenty-five-cent cigars. I smoked ten-centers and that's what I got. Both boxes, incidentally, came from the large number of gift cigars sent to the President that were stacked up in his study. I guess Mr. Coolidge figured that if I smoked ten-cent cigars, I wouldn't appreciate anything better. . . .

Almost every White House family has some pet that becomes well known to the nation. In the case of the Coolidges, it was the handsome white collie dog. . . . The collie was best known, perhaps, because it was included in a portrait of Mrs. Coolidge done by Howard Chandler Christy. The President liked the painting and decided it would be nice to send photographs of it to their friends. One was sent to the man who had given the collie to the President. Mr. Coolidge got a telegram in reply: "Fine picture of dog. Send more photographs." . . .

The President didn't miss any political bets either, for all of his dead-pan approach to publicity hoop-la. He had a temper that could make itself felt in high places, but he always felt a strong sympathy for the ordinary citizen and frequently went out of his way to perform some little act of thoughtfulness for a stranger.

One Sunday morning when I was at the office trying to catch up with a heavy flood of mail, he came over from the White House and stood beside my desk while I opened a large pile of letters. One of them was a special delivery letter from a woman who wanted to know what church the President would attend that day and at what time he would be there. She explained that she was in Washington only for a few days and that she wanted her small son to get a glimpse of the President while he was in the Capital, because it would be something he would remember always and could tell his friends about. She asked whether it would be possible to telephone her at her hotel and tell her which church Mr. Coolidge would attend.

I handed him the letter and he read it carefully. Without saying anything, he picked up a pencil and wrote: "Phone 10:30 A.M. Monday." He handed the notation to me and went abruptly away. Such notes were typical of Mr. Coolidge, and I understood that he meant for me to telephone the woman and tell her to bring her son to the White House on Monday at 10:30 A.M. for a visit with the President. This I did, and the delighted mother and son were received by Mr. Coolidge.

When Mr. Coolidge's term ended, he just sort of faded out of the White House without any formal good-bys, and Herbert Hoover took over. I, for one, was sorry to see Mr. Coolidge go, because it seemed to me that his departure marked the end of a chapter in our history. He was probably the last of our modern-era Presidents who was able to give the impression of avoiding the extreme mental and physical strains of the office. This was due both to the period in which he served and to his temperament, although it was difficult to tell just what tensions were at work behind that New England façade.

He believed, however, that a man was inefficient if he failed to get through his allotted work each day. Mr. Coolidge always got through his. He didn't like noise or hoop-la, and he didn't like sudden and drastic changes—the kind of changes that we were heading for even if we could not then see them. He was, perhaps, a little old-fashioned, and, as I hope I've made clear, I liked him, and I believe he liked me. I never laughed heartily at his jokes—just enough to let him know I got the point. He seemed to like that. He may even have realized that very few of his jokes were worth more than a mild chuckle, but I doubt it.

A Day at the White House

By FRENCH STROTHER

French Strother was an Associate Editor of the magazine *World's Work* in 1924 at the time the full text of this article was originally published. Mr. Strother also acted as an administrative assistant to Herbert Hoover, both before and during Mr. Hoover's Presidential years.

THE DAY'S WORK of the President begins at nine o'clock when he appears at his desk in the Executive Offices at the west end of the White House. The oval room is large and quiet, and is decorated in soothing tones of pale and dark green. The light comes from a great curving bay window, its southern exposure giving out on the lawn of the White House grounds, and looking toward the Washington Monument, which towers above the trees of the Mall. President Coolidge sits at a mahogany desk with his back to the window and facing a cheery fireplace. In the middle of the wall to his left hand is the door from the secretary's office, through which his callers come. A corresponding door to his right leads to the Cabinet room. . . .

The President's office is as quiet as a drawing room, but it is surrounded by a life as tense and pulsating as that which surrounds the office of any great business executive.

Every new President produces a distinctive change in the atmosphere that surrounds this wing of the White House. . . . The Executive Offices of the White House today are more like the executive offices of the head of a great business than they have ever been in modern times. The President regards himself as a servant of the people, employed for one sole purpose: namely, to transact their public business. He transacts it like a business man. . . .

From nine to ten, he dictates his personal correspondence. Twice a week the Director of the Budget reports to him at 9:30 o'clock. From ten to one is a continuous succession of appointments: a committee chairman from the House has ten minutes for consultation; Chairman Adams of the Republican National Committee has fifteen for a political discussion; a Metropolitan Opera tenor has two minutes for a handshake and felicitations; Senator Pepper has ten for a suggestion of counsel for the oil lease investigation; Mr. Garcia of San Juan, three, in which to present a beautifully bound volume of Porto Rican views from the President's Island admirers; a delegation of six Masons from a Western city, five minutes to invite the President to lay a cornerstone (the President, by the way, belongs to no secret order); Secretary of Labor Davis, four minutes, in which to present a visiting delegation of sixty-five marine engineers—the list can be extended indefinitely by the reader, with the use of a little imagination, with almost the certainty that he cannot make a mistake, because, in the course of a month, practically every conceivable kind of man, woman, and child appears at the White House on "business with the President" which to them is of first importance.

Shortly before one o'clock a line of perhaps a hundred people has been formed in the corridor. These frankly say they want only to shake the President's hand. The doors in the corners of his private office are opened, Secret Service men station themselves at each, the President takes his stand in the middle of the room with Mr. Slemp [the Secretary to the President] at his left, and the line comes in the left door, passes the President, and goes out at the right. Each visitor's name is inquired by Mr. Slemp, who, in turn, introduces him to the President. He greets each with a smile and a cheerful "How do you do?" or "Delighted to meet you!"—expressed with the indescribable New England twang, all the words of each salutation being fully and slowly pronounced in the same tone, except the last word, which rises sharply in pitch and in a staccato emphasis.

The reception over, the President repairs to the main part of the White House for luncheon. Usually he is back at his desk by two, or a very little later. He has few appointments in the afternoon; these hours are kept free for calls by members of the Cabinet and for conferences with members of Congress who come at his request. A certain amount of time is left for the signing of commissions and documents, for which the President's signature is required by law (among antiquated absurdities in this class are provisions that he must sign the commissions of notaries public of the District of Columbia and all wills of Indians who are government charges). Photographs are autographed and the mail of the day signed late in the afternoon. A significant touch here: the President never signs anything in ignorance of its contents; he is no more perfunctory in this detail than he is in any other occupation.

An innovation in the day's work is just now being introduced. The President wishes not merely to dispose of business as it arises. He wishes in addition to make an organized study of all the great national problems. For this purpose he has made out a list of the subjects he wishes to investigate, and Mr. Slemp has allotted certain days to each, upon which the best-informed men in these subjects are summoned to Washington from all parts of the country, arriving at scheduled hours at the White House for intensive discussion, at the request of the President. In a few months this system will put him in possession of the best information and opinion of the country on current problems that organized effort can provide. . . .

The day's work ends at—when it ends. If he is fortunate, it may be at 4:30 o'clock, when he can go for a walk or for a horseback ride, or, in the summer time, perhaps start for an overnight cruise on the *Mayflower*. If less fortunate, it may not end until six o'clock, with barely time left to prepare for dinner. In another sense, distinctive of Mr. Coolidge, it practically never ends. As has been said before . . . , his outstanding characteristic is hard, purposeful, continuous thinking. From this he rarely rests. The President's hours of ease (such few as they are) come after he leaves the Executive Offices, at 5:30 or six in the evening, until he retires at about 10:30; and from 6:30 in the morning, when he arises, until he returns to his desk at the west end of the White House at nine. An hour for luncheon may sometimes be added to this picture, when he may share his simple noonday meal with family friends who are house guests, or with old-time neighbors from Massachusetts, who have called at his office during the morning to pay their respects. Oftener, however, luncheon is a business conference as well. This, indeed, is true of many dinners.

The President of the United States has a good deal of official entertaining to do, and the large formal dinners at the White House are as much a part of the day's work as the routine of his office. These formal gatherings need only be mentioned in passing, as they have no reference to Mr. Coolidge as distinguished from any other President, because their occurrence and details are formalities of official tradition and do not change from administration to administration.

The evenings at the White House which do bear the stamp of President Coolidge's individuality are those when only one or two guests are present and no official business is involved. These intimate evenings are almost as simple and informal as though they were in his former modest home at Northampton. The guests are nearly always invited verbally. The dinner hour is seven o'clock. The guest arrives at the main north entrance. The porte-cochère and veranda are dimly lighted from above; a small group of reporters stand in the shadow of one of the towering Grecian columns that support the portico, waiting for the emergence of a public man known to be in conference with the President. Two policemen are on guard.

As the guest approaches the great glass doors, they are opened for him by an usher, who asks his name and has evidently been forewarned of his coming. The colored doorman, with a Virginian accent and idiom, smilingly ask[s] if the guest will "rest yoh hat an' coat." Relieved of these, the guest is passed on to another usher, and by him into the Red Room to await the President's descent from the family quarters on the second floor. In a few minutes the slightly clanging sound of an elevator door floats in from the reception hall, and a moment later the President enters the Red Room, followed immediately by Mrs. Coolidge. His firm handshake is accompanied by a shy smile and a salutation, brief, but conveying in its intonation more of welcome than the printed words can convey. . . .

The visitor is at once introduced to Mrs. Coolidge. A more complete contrast between two people, both in appearance and manner, would be hard to imagine. The President's very fair complexion, with the red showing very plainly through (he abundantly freckles in summer); his blue-gray eyes; his thin, straight, and sandy hair; his prominent nose, and slightly rounded shoulders, are in direct contrast to the corresponding features of Mrs. Coolidge. Her complexion is olive; her eyes large and dark brown; her hair abundant, wavy, black just lightly powdered with gray, her nose has an almost jaunty tilt, and her carriage is easy and erect.

The mouths remain to be described. The President's is most unusual, seeming to be divided laterally into thirds. The central section is a straight horizonal line, flanked on either side by a drop at a sharp angle of almost forty-five degrees to the corners. The upper lip is fairly full; the lower so thin that it shows no red at all when the mouth is closed. Mrs. Coolidge's mouth is wide, the lips full, and, like her dancing eyes, expresses instantly her rapid shift from mood to mood. Strangely enough, in view of the popular conception of their characters, it is the President, and not Mrs. Coolidge, who has a dimple in the point of the chin. The impression of the two to-

gether is that the President is a nervously alert man, constantly under the perfect control of a firm will, and that Mrs. Coolidge "hasn't
a nerve in her body," and therefore gives rein to the graceful vivacity of movement characteristic of a woman in perfect health and
full of the joy of living.

The party moves at once to the dining room. It would be hard to
find a man of simpler habit than the President, but he evidently feels
the obligation to preserve the tradition of official etiquette, so that
he is punctilious in following the prescribed rules of precedence inherited from generations of his predecessors. At the door of the
great paneled dining room, Rob Roy, the big, pure-white collie from
Wisconsin, comes bounding across the room to greet him. The President's face lights with pleasure, and he returns the salutation with
affectionate pats and "good doggie." After this exchange of greetings,
the President leads Rob Roy to the fireplace to "charge" on the
hearth, while the dinner is in progress. The meal itself is of the
simplest—a clear soup, a cutlet with string beans and potatoes, to-
mato salad, ice cream, cake, and coffee.

The conversation is about anything and everything except the
President's work. Never since her marriage has Mrs. Coolidge discussed his business with her husband. I venture to surmise that she
adopted this practice deliberately for his sake. Few men concentrate
so intensely upon their work as the President, and this has been his
habit since boyhood. Mrs. Coolidge must have felt that her duty as
his wife was to make home an absolute refuge from this intense preoccupation. She is as conspicuously a "social being" as her husband
is not. Lively spirits, an irrepressible instinct for fun, a gift for ready
and entertaining conversation, warmth of feeling and the capacity
to express it—these are qualities universally attributed to her, and
verified upon the most casual meeting. They cannot but be a relief
and solace to her silent companion, who has always lived a life of
intense intellectual activity, accompanied by the emotional strain
peculiar to men of strong feeling, held in constant repression.

Mrs. Coolidge and the guest do most of the talking, the President
supplying an occasional comment—here a fact needed to complete
a sentence of his wife's, there a question of anxious concern about

her welfare when she describes a slight accident to herself, and again a humorous, sometimes quizzical, commentary upon a bit of her narrative. . . .

The conversation drifts around to the boys, who are away at school and keenly missed. Mrs. Coolidge remarks that it has been two years since the boys were with them except for vacations, and the President, with a characteristic instinct for exactness, corrects the figure to "three years." The wonders of radio are discussed, and some one remarks that an expert has said that the President has an unusually good radio voice, that it—the speaker gropes for the technical phrase. The President supplies it: it is "cuts through."

As dessert time approaches, Rob Roy slips from the hearthstone to the President's side, to remind him that he expects his customary share in the meal at this point; and the President sends the butler for the dog's regular evening allotment of sweetmeats. Dinner over, the party adjourns upstairs, Rob Roy occupying the seat in the elevator and accompanying Mrs. Coolidge to the library, while the President adjourns to the study for a cigar and a glance at the news of the day.

The study is a very cheerful room. The big fireplace, the easy chairs, the walls crowded with paintings of American historical events and characters, an enormous desk covered with books, papers, and magazines, flanked at the right by a silken American flag and at the left by the President's standard—the room is really gay with color and warmth. The news is provided for the President in this way: the principal American newspapers are carefully scanned by members of the secretarial staff, and all news of interest to the President is clipped and pasted on uniform large sheets of yellow paper. All the clippings on a particular subject are put together and the sheets fastened at the corner with a clasp. By this device the President can in a few moments get a quick picture of newspaper opinion on any particular subject as reflected in headlines, news articles, and editorial comment. . . .

The scene shifts to the library, where a member of the staff has produced for Mrs. Coolidge's inspection some old photographs of the interior of the White House before it was altered under the

Roosevelt régime. There are dozens of these pictures. The President examines them closely and with occasional amusement at antiquities of dress and furnishings in some of them. Four pictures engage the President's attention longer than the others. Of these, two are photographs in which children and animals are the center of interest. The third is of a stairway which was removed when the dining room was enlarged to its present proportions. Its interest seems to lie in the challenge to the mind to work out the problem of how the change was made to acquire the additional space. The fourth picture, the most pondered of the four, is of an office with several men working at desks, in a room which is now a part of the living quarters, but was then one of the executive offices. Its appeal may have lain in its evidences of order and application to work—distinctive characteristics of the President himself.

The books at the White House are a casual miscellany. The President does not read general literature either for pleasure or cultural development. As a young man he liked fiction and read a little. He liked poetry, especially the New England poets, and read them a good deal. But since he first began the practice of law in Northampton, his whole thought has been of his work. In his own language, "When I was a lawyer, my nose was always in a law book; and when I got into public life, I had to read public documents to keep up with my work." It may be doubted whether, from a young man to the present, the President has read more than a few works of general literature, or in any books outside the field of history, economics, and biography, these being directly related to his public service.

The President has no recreations of the usual kind. He does not play cards or other games that while the time away.

It was suggested at the beginning of this article, that his hours of ease are "such as they are." All too often his evenings are interrupted two or three times by the advent of callers upon emergency business. Their resort is the study; and in its evening quiet, many of the President's most important official words and deeds are uttered and done.

Such hours of ease as he now has—all too broken—are devoted wholly to the companionship of his wife and friends. Mrs. Coolidge, by nature and by choice, makes these hours as different as can be from the strain of the day. Naturally vivacious and fun-loving, she has, besides, a quite exceptional social gift and a fine mind, both of which have been educated by experience, wide reading, and abundant social life, so that the atmosphere into which the President relaxes from his day's work is one of sunny warmth, agreeable and intelligent conversation, and a homelike naturalness of spirit that conform perfectly with his own simplicity of character.

The President's habits of repose are based upon the sound old maxim, "Early to bed, early to rise." Nothing is allowed to interfere with this part of his daily regimen; and to this severe regularity of sleep his constant good health may be in part ascribed. At a quarter past ten, the guest is conscious that the President is growing sleepy. To intimate that he is aware of the President's habits, he professes an ignorance of the White House etiquette of departure, which is briefly explained and the conversation continues. In a few moments the President declares it is time for him to go to bed. The guest rises, but realizes that the President should indicate his wishes by rising first, so resumes his seat. The President's eye twinkles a humorous, silent signal of sympathetic comprehension, and a moment later he rises, and the guest follows suit. The adieux are made, and the guest departs into the night. Fifteen minutes later, the President is sound asleep.

Clothes and the President

By MARY RANDOLPH

For seven years, during the entire Coolidge administration and part of President Hoover's as well, Mary Randolph filled the position of Social Secretary at the White House.

I NEVER KNEW any man more interested in his wife's clothes than Mr. Coolidge, and the handsomer and more elaborate Mrs. Coolidge's dresses were, the better he liked them. He was fond of bright colors, conspicuous ornaments, glittering beads. Usually careful of expenditures—unbelievably economical in many ways—he not only spared no expense, he gave way to wild extravagance when it came to the question of Mrs. Coolidge's clothes.

Believe it or not, he never wanted her to wear the same dress twice to a State Reception! I have seen him stop beside the bed where her gorgeous dress for the evening was laid out—perhaps a glittering lamé or a handsome heavy silk, brocaded in velvet—and have heard him say tersely:

"You've worn that dress before."

And I've heard Mrs. Coolidge reply:

"Yes, of course I have. It's a very handsome dress and I like to wear it."

But he would have given her a new and expensive gown for every State occasion. Nothing was too much, no expense too great. This was the one extravagance of an otherwise overconservative, somewhat inhibited, and notably economical man.

Mrs. Coolidge often said she meant to have a dress like the one Martha Washington wears in the portrait hanging in the White House—with a quilted satin petticoat, an overdress with panniers and elbow sleeves, lace ruffles, and a lace fichu. She never got round to it, though she had many lovely dresses, choosing for one State Reception a heavy white satin brocade, very simply made and fastened at the waistline with one pearl ornament. This dress had a graceful skirt down to the instep and a tremendously long "court train," and it was almost finished—in fact, we were in the midst of the final fitting, Mrs. Coolidge before the tall mirror, the fitter on her knees adjusting the train, and I standing near by—when President Coolidge strolled into the room.

"What do you think of it?" asked Mrs. Coolidge.

After a long, critical survey, taking in every detail:

"Very handsome dress," he said; and then to our horror he calmly walked up the long white brocaded train which swept for yards upon the floor, putting one foot deliberately before the other as though pacing off the length of the material!

There was a concerted shriek from Mrs. Coolidge and the fitter, who flung herself on all fours toward the precious train.

"Mr. President," I said sternly, with the fearless frankness of long association, "get right straight off that train!"

Apparently meek as a lamb, but with a twinkle in his eye, he did "get right off," sauntering slowly out of the room, while the almost fainting dressmaker looked to see if any damage had been done.

"Oh!" she gasped. "There is not another inch of this material to be had! But it's all right; I can't find a spot on it."

Often, walking in the late afternoon through the shopping district, President Coolidge would see in a window some dress that took his fancy—usually with vivid ribbons on it, or some other dash of brilliant color—and promptly he would order it sent to the White House on approval. Sometimes Mrs. Coolidge liked his choice and often she did not. I remember a black velvet with a great many scarlet streamers hanging down the front from neck to hem. Bringing this dress to my desk, "What do you think of *this* that the President has had sent up for me to see?" asked Mrs. Coolidge.

Gathering up the streamers in my hand and tucking them out of sight, "It wouldn't be bad without these," I said.

"Oh," said Mrs. Coolidge, "but that's what he likes about it; *that* is why it took his eye!"

"Mercy," I said. "What can you do?"

"I think it is two sizes too big," said Mrs. Coolidge, "and we will just tell him that it is too large to be altered successfully."

She never knew what would be sent home for her to try on, but his interest was both flattering and touching.

Very observant and particular was Mr. Coolidge about all women's clothes, and Mrs. Coolidge never wore the very short skirts of 1926-27, when evening entertainments were shorn of their grace and elegance by the appearance of ladies of all shapes scantily clad in gorgeous materials, reaching barely to the knee—gnarled or dimpled, as the case might be—or only a little below it.

The Coolidges usually took quite a party of people down the river with them on week-end trips on the *Mayflower,* and one attractive young Washington matron, with her husband, was a frequent guest—Mrs. C. C. Glover, Jr. Pretty and extremely bright as she is, Mr. Coolidge always liked to talk to her. He was sitting by her side one evening after dinner, and she told me that her short dress had worried her because, when she sat down, it had a way of creeping up; and so she was nervously twitching at the end of her skirt, vainly trying to make it cover her knees. She had no idea that the President noticed it, but after a few moments, taking his cigar out of his mouth, he dryly remarked, in his nasal drawl:

"What *yeou* need is a rug."

"What a thing to have to tell my grandchildren," said Mrs. Glover, "when they ask me some day, 'and what did the President say to you, grandmamma?' "

A Naval Aide's Report

By WILSON BROWN

During three separate tours of duty at the White House, Wilson Brown acted as naval aide to four Presidents, beginning with Mr. Coolidge in 1926.

A T TWILIGHT on a pleasant August afternoon in the year 1926, Calvin Coolidge, thirtieth President of the United States, sat in a rocking chair at the side of his Vermont farmhouse. He had arrived at Plymouth only a few hours before, after a day's journey from his summer camp in the Adirondacks. It was his first visit home since the burial of his father in the local graveyard the winter before. Then heavy snow in Vermont made all travel difficult, and piercing wind and cold lashed the funeral cortege. Today a green and smiling countryside welcomed Vermont's most distinguished citizen. His purpose in this return was to revisit the grave of his father and his beloved younger son, whose recent tragic death also seemed only yesterday.

Today, after all the hurly-burly of high office, President and Mrs. Coolidge could inspect the house he had inherited from his father, and they had it to themselves, attended only by an austere spinster neighbor who acted as their local housekeeper. Except for a few who remained in the neighborhood on duty, the Presidential following of secretaries, Secret Service, telegraph and telephone operators, press and photographers had moved on another fifteen miles to the hotel in the neighboring town of Woodstock.

From where he sat, Calvin Coolidge could look across the country road to his pasture land that leads away to a green valley and hills beyond. He could also see what went on at the crossroads country store where he was born, fifty yards up the road. . . . At the moment it had become the headquarters of the duty section of his staff, and there a curious crowd had quickly assembled beyond a cordon fixed by the State Police to prevent further encroachment on the Presidential privacy.

The President had been very grumpy all day on the trip to Plymouth and had refused Mrs. Coolidge's earnest pleas to address crowds that had waited hours for a single glimpse of him; and at times he refused even to stand up where he could be seen. It was clear to all of us that we should leave him alone unless we had something important to deliver. It fell to me, the new man, to be the first intruder.

It was a completely strange environment for me. I had taken command of the Presidential yacht, *Mayflower*, and had assumed the duties of Naval Aide only a few months before. I had seen very little of President and Mrs. Coolidge. At the few White House receptions and during trips on the *Mayflower* I had found them friendly but very official and formal. On board the *Mayflower* I knew what my duties were and how to do them, but in the mountains of Vermont I had no intimation of what was expected of me beyond the generally accepted requirement "to be on hand in case something turns up." The recent death of President Harding had put everyone around the White House on the alert for other possible emergencies, and I was on my toes. My navy-blue uniform with aiguillettes, which custom required me to wear, seemed particularly inappropriate to the surroundings. It collected all of the dust of all of the country roads in spite of most diligent brushing. I felt conspicuous and a little silly.

I was staying with the nearest neighbor (Farmer Brown, the President called him) and, in order to be of some slight service, I had constituted myself a link between the President and our telegraph operators established in the country store with a direct wire to Washington.

The Coolidges had not enjoyed many minutes of quiet before the Washington operator reported that he had no further business and asked permission to sign off for the night. Reluctant as I was to disturb the tranquillity of the peaceful moment, I thought the President might be waiting for the all clear from Washington, and I therefore passed through the police cordon, walked to the porch rail, made my report of all quiet, and asked if he had any more business.

"Come up and sit," said the President.

"Oh, no thank you, Mr. President," I said, "I don't want to intrude, but thought you might like to know there is no more business from Washington tonight."

"Come up and sit," he repeated a little more emphatically.

Notwithstanding the command quality of his invitation, Calvin Coolidge, by some intangible quality of voice, expression, and gesture, made me feel that he did not resent my interruption, but, on the contrary, realizing perhaps my predicament, was glad of an opportunity to show me special kindness in a way that would be noted by others. We sat in silence for some time, but it was not an uncomfortable silence. The mere fact that Mrs. Coolidge did not feel it necessary to talk was reassuring. No one understood her husband's moods as well as she, and she always came promptly to the rescue when the situation required. After a while Mr. Coolidge made an occasional comment—about the weather, the beauty of the view, and how fond he was of it.

"Are you comfortable at Farmer Brown's?" he asked, and I said yes. Later, as the light faded, he spoke again. "Perhaps you'd like to see the house. Most visitors do."

He led me through the lower floor, pointing out where his father used to sit, where he used to study his lessons as a boy, where his father stood when he swore him in as President of the United States.

After a few halting comments, I thanked him and said I'd better go. Was there anything I could do? We were passing through the kitchen toward the porch. Mr. Coolidge opened the icebox door, inspected its well-filled contents and said, "Well, Momma, anything you want Captain Brown to get from the store before they close?" But Mrs. Coolidge, it turned out, was all stocked.

We remained at Plymouth for several days, during which Calvin Coolidge went tranquilly about the business of inspecting his heritage—house, barns, outbuildings, equipment and land. He allowed but few interruptions—now and then an occasional visitor too important to be refused the door and, as a sop to the press, posing for a few pictures. He put on dungarees and a large farmer's straw hat for these and was shown doing farm chores in a rather unconvincing manner.

At this time there was little in Calvin Coolidge's physical appearance to indicate a farm background. He seemed too frail ever to have managed the tasks of farm labor or even ever to have taken part in school or college athletics. An oval-shaped head and clear-cut profile suggested Anglo-Saxon ancestry. A thin neck, sloping shoulders, rather shambling gait, suggested a boy who had never found time to play, rather than one accustomed to outdoor life. He may have chopped wood, fed the chickens and milked the cow as a young boy; but I could not see him handling the plow or the hoe. Yet there was no pretense in Calvin Coolidge's make-up. He wished the American people to see him and his neighbors as they were. He was proud of a strain of Indian blood, of the hardihood of his ancestors in surviving the rigors of northern winter, of the God-fearing principles of their lives.

While the Coolidges were intent upon their own affairs, the staff and members of the press loafed in the shade of a fine old tree just outside the country store—pitching pennies, spinning yarns, discussing everything under the sun. For all of us there were many dull hours. One afternoon I took off down the lane away from the crowd, within sight of the house and store where I could be called if needed, to become completely absorbed in reading one of the four long volumes of Beveridge's life of John Marshall.

I was aroused from my concentration by a familiar voice at my elbow saying in clipped tones, "Well, Captain, studying navigation?" As I started to climb down from the rail fence where I was perched, he headed me off with, "Don't disturb yourself. I'm just looking around and wondered what you were so interested in." When I told him, his comment was, "A fine book. Every American ought to read it. You couldn't spend your time to better advantage. Go ahead with your reading,"—and walked off.

Years later when I praised the Beveridge work to Franklin Roosevelt, he disagreed completely, denouncing the books as "fusty volumes that thought only of property rights and worried little about human rights and public welfare." This opposite judgment of the merits of Beveridge's work is an excellent example of the basic differences in the political philosophy of Calvin Coolidge and that of Franklin Roosevelt. . . .

When Mr. Coolidge was Vice-President he and Mrs. Coolidge were obliged by the social requirements of the office to attend official or semiofficial dinners nearly every night. His puritanical bearing, forming as it did so amusing a contrast to the gayer members of the free and easy Harding administration, led to many anecdotes. One, for example, had it that a lady who commiserated with the Vice-President for having to endure so much dining out got this laconic comment from him: "Gotta eat somewhere." I suppose this tale was manufactured, like most of the world's best "true" anecdotes, although I have heard it countless times.

But when Mr. Coolidge became President his habits changed. Henceforward he was at pains to avoid private social engagements —and all the entanglements they might involve—and keep everything official. At the same time formal entertaining at the White House reached a new high level, and so it was when I first had a part in it. Presidents Harding and Coolidge had reinstituted the full schedule of White House formal dinners and receptions initiated during the administration of Theodore Roosevelt but interrupted for a time by World War I and the illness of President Wilson.

Every month there were about five dinners and an equal number of receptions. This meant a big party about every week during the winter, so that the main floor of the White House was in a constant state of activity, with furniture and rugs and flowers steadily moving in and out. There was a correct and established way of doing everything in the White House and everything had to be done according to that code. Each move for every ceremony was rehearsed with West Point precision by the protocol officer of the State Department, the head usher, Ike Hoover, and the Army and Navy aides. All hands, including President and Mrs. Coolidge, were made to toe the line. Strangely enough, that plain Yankee, with all of his real love for simplicity, approved the ritual.

The gossip around Washington was that Mr. Coolidge ate his dinner in bored silence and refused to be drawn into conversation by the most charming ladies. . . . [But Mr.] Coolidge was not a man to be deliberately rude to a dinner guest. I have sat at his table at a good many formal dinners and even more smaller luncheons, and I have never seen him ignore his partners. He was of course never loquacious and when pressed—especially by gushy matrons—would clam up completely. Nor was he niggardly, as many wits suggested. The Coolidge board fairly groaned and there were many courses. According to present-day standards there was too much to eat. Wine was, of course, never served as Calvin Coolidge would not temporize with the law even though he did not approve of Prohibition. An invitation was much sought after by all who did not, like the Cabinet, get too much of it.

State receptions were carried out with the same pomp as the dinners—lavish floral decorations, Marine Orchestra, aides in full uniform. The guests would begin arriving a full hour before the time set for the reception, for several thousand would have been asked. Except for a few seniors who led the line, the others would form in the order of their arrival—filling the East Room, the lower corridor and the stairway leading to the main floor from the lower corridor. The Cabinet and their ladies assembled in the Blue Room. At the appointed hour the President and Mrs. Coolidge would make their formal appearance to the strains of "Hail to the Chief!" Preceded by the aides, they would descend the stairs, normally kept closed with iron gates, to enter the lower hall in the midst of the assembled guests. The stairs are wide and graceful and their use lent a faint air of royal pomp or, at least, Viennese opera to this republican soirée. The President and his lady then passed through the crowd in the main hall by a passage kept clear by the junior aides, into the Blue Room where the Cabinet was assembled and up to the ropes that fixed the position of the receiving line.

The President's job of the evening would then begin—shaking hands with more than 2,000 guests. It was quite evident to all that Mr. Coolidge wanted only to get this manual marathon over with as quickly as possible, and he combined with his handshake a perceptible pull toward Mrs. Coolidge on his right. If the passer paused to chat, as many would, the pull was more powerful. But any apparent lack of cordiality in the President was counterbalanced by Mrs. Coolidge's charm and friendliness. She really appeared to enjoy seeing people, calling by name without prompting all she had ever met before. Mrs. Coolidge never seemed to tire and would be as gay and sparkling at the end as at the beginning.

This was frankly not so with the President or his two aides. General Sherwood Cheney and I alternated every fifteen minutes, standing on the President's left and announcing to him the name of each passerby. The guest would give us his name and we would repeat it to the President. We would turn the head to the left; concentrate on hearing and grasping the name; turn the head to the right and announce the name; then turn back to catch the next name; and so continue without pause until relieved. The faster the line moved the faster we had to turn, listen, turn, speak, as if in a squirrel cage. The head would get dizzy, the neck would ache. It all appeared very serious to Mr. Coolidge, and we could sense his annoyance when we bungled a name. When I had the job to do years later with Franklin Roosevelt, who had the added torture of standing for a long time on braces, he was the gayest of us all and joshed General "Pa" Watson and me when we called a wrong name.

After one reception General Cheney and I had preceded the President and Mrs. Coolidge in their march to the second floor, which was always the finale of the evening. We started down the stairs as they turned toward their apartment; but, suddenly remembering that we had a question to ask about next day's duties, we turned back just in time to see the President and his wife, believing themselves to be alone, solemnly dancing a minuet with exaggerated bows and curtsies. Perhaps he didn't take his receptions as seriously as we thought.

Once I remember hearing an earnest lady admirer tell President Coolidge that she did not see how he could bear up under all his pressing responsibilities and that she prayed often for his health and guidance. Did he not often find his burden more than he could endure?

"Oh, I don't know," said the President. "There are only so many hours in the day, and one can only do the best he can in the time he's got. When I was Mayor of Northampton, I was pretty busy most of the time, and I don't seem to be much busier here. I just have to settle different kinds of things."

On board the *Mayflower* we would have little preparation to make except to check that all was shipshape, to order a huge supply of flowers from the White House greenhouse and large quantities of food. On sailing day we would give everything a final polish, and get our stores aboard, including a supply of newspapers, magazines, and books. Then we would single up the lines to the dock, and be ready to get under way the moment the President stepped aboard.

Sailing was generally at eleven thirty, but by eleven we would all be on deck in dress uniform, the crew manning the rail, band and Marine Guard paraded clear of the gangway, sideboys within hail, stewards on the dock ready to bring baggage on board for the passengers. The Commandant of the Navy Yard would come on the dock with a supporting cast of reporters, photographers, and a group of curious onlookers. The guests would then begin to arrive. Members of the Cabinet receive the honors prescribed by Navy regulations: attention on the bugle, the side piped, ruffles and the appropriate march, guard at present arms, sideboys and all hands at salute. Most wives are visibly pleased and excited by this demonstration of their husband's importance. Most husbands pretend to be bored, but are secretly delighted. I would shake hands with the guests at the gangway, escort them aft, and turn them over to a junior officer to be shown their rooms. All guests then assembled on the spacious afterdeck to await the arrival of President and Mrs. Coolidge.

When we got word from the Navy Yard gate that the President's cars had passed through, ship's company would jump to stations and, as the cars drew alongside, would render full Presidential honors—except that the twenty-one-gun salute was usually dispensed with. The Presidential flag would then be broken at the main truck, the gangway hauled aboard, lines cast off, and the *Mayflower* would steam majestically down river, graceful as a swan. The President would walk aft to greet his guests and sit with them for a time on deck, where all could see the shore lines unfold and the beautiful outline of the city of Washington fade away astern.

A most important incident of the departure ceremony was always the arrival of the head steward on deck with the President's yachting cap. This had been purchased by Captain Adolphus Andrews, my predecessor, at Brooks Brothers, a smart and expensive outfitter which Mr. Coolidge had never patronized—he visited a modest tailor and was scandalized to learn that Andrews would pay $150 for a suit of clothes. It was a well-designed, plain yachting cap with simple black visor, but the best that money could buy. Mr. Coolidge was very much pleased with it and wore it on deck at all times. . . .

Because the *Mayflower* dining saloon was below decks, the President usually delayed luncheon and kept his guests on deck until after we had passed Mount Vernon. Thus they could take part in the ceremonies prescribed by the Navy for all American ships passing Washington's tomb—parading the guard, attention on the bugle, tolling the ship's bell, all hands at salute. The simplicity of Mount Vernon as seen from the river, the fine sweep of the shore line at that point, the emotional effect of the ceremony will not be forgotten by many who have cruised on the *Mayflower*.

After quite a hearty tea, when conversation would begin to lag, Mrs. Coolidge generally announced that it was time to dress for dinner. Sometimes I was invited for dinner but more often not, as I had responsibilities on the bridge. I would say to the President that, if he approved, I would anchor for the night off Piney Point at the mouth of the Potomac. He always said, "Very well," as I knew he would, for that was the routine he liked. Then, quite early, he would go to bed, as would most of the guests. The ship then set a security watch and the Secret Service would keep close guard at the

Presidential cabin door. All enjoyed the sea breezes and all except the watch standers would have a good night's rest.

While the *Mayflower* often enabled President Coolidge to escape the cares of state, I am sorry to confess that she and I caused him discomfort and embarrassment on the occasion when he was persuaded to hold a fleet review. At that period in our history the Navy was very much concerned about the already evident effects of the limitation of naval armament. The military clique of Japan, attacking "the indignity of the 5-5-3 ratio," was stirring up strong anti-American feeling. We believed that they were building ships and fortifying the Caroline and Marshall Islands in violation of treaties—and yet we continued to haggle with Britain about how many cruisers each should have and, to show our good faith, destroyed on the ways thousands of tons of ships which, had they been completed, might have deterred Japan from ever making her attack on Pearl Harbor. Fearing the worst, the Navy Department saw in a fleet review an opportunity to throw the spotlight of publicity on the need for more ships and more positive action. They also wanted to demonstrate to the President personally some of our most evident weaknesses.

I think President Coolidge never had much faith in limitation of armaments as an instrument for peace; but he felt that, having gone so far, we must give it a fair trial. He was therefore reluctant to encourage any naval building at that time. Also, being a poor sailor, he was very fearful of being laughed at if he had the bad luck to be seasick during the review. But, after a good deal of discussion and with the aid of some members of Congress, he was finally persuaded that if we anchored the *Mayflower* in Lynnhaven Roads, well inside the Virginia Capes, there was very little chance of any motion and the fleet could parade by on its way to anchorage farther up the Roads. I pointed out that we could leave Washington as usual and make our customary two-day trip, except that instead of anchoring for the night at Piney Point we would keep under way at night and be anchored the second day for review. Finally President Coolidge reluctantly consented. There was a good deal of preliminary publicity.

Weather conditions looked favorable. We left on schedule; but, alas, during the night a heavy ground swell began piling in through the Capes and when we anchored, the *Mayflower* had a roll—not a heavy roll, but heavy enough to embarrass others besides Mr. Coolidge—the one possible weather condition we had dreaded. The President was cross (as who isn't when he's seasick?) and stayed in his bunk most of the morning. In accordance with his instructions I entertained a specially selected group of press and photographers in the President's dining room, and, at his expense, gave them a very superior stand-up luncheon. We told them that they had the run of the ship except for a small portion of the deck which was roped off to provide privacy for the Presidential party. They were asked to keep clear of that space, and I assigned an officer and two Marine orderlies to be sure there was no slip-up.

When the fleet flagship came in sight leading the column, a queasy Coolidge roused from his misery and his bunk and came to the bridge with his binoculars and yachting cap. During a full half hour he posed for the photographers, looking sternly through the long signal glass, pointing to each ship as she came abeam, returning salutes endlessly while trying to stand at attention and steady himself against the roll with the unengaged hand. He played his part correctly throughout the picture-taking ordeal. Then, when all the battleships had passed, Mr. Coolidge said he would go aft to the roped-off area and watch the rest from there. Behind the afterdeck house and out of sight of prying eyes, he sank into a sofa.

Presently the fleet commander, Admiral Hughes, came aboard with a considerable staff, and a photographer slipped along with them unnoticed as the procession moved aft. Thus he was able to sneak a snapshot of Mr. Coolidge seated disconsolately on the sofa, grim-lipped, clearly dreaming only of terra firma and an end to his malaise. That rather comic stolen picture was given greater publicity than almost any other. Calvin Coolidge never uttered one word of reproach to any of us for causing his embarrassment. But neither did he give any support to a naval building program.

A Congressional Viewpoint

By BERTRAND H. SNELL

Bertrand H. Snell was a Member of Congress from New York from 1915 to 1939, serving as minority leader of the House from 1931 until the time of his retirement. He had been graduated from Amherst College in 1894, a year ahead of Calvin Coolidge.

I FIRST BECAME acquainted with Calvin Coolidge when he was a freshman in Amherst College, but I never was really closely associated with him until he became President. During that time I was Chairman of the Rules Committee of the House of Representatives. I saw him almost daily in connection with important legislation.

He was one of the finest men to work with that I have ever known, and he was always willing to give consideration to the point of view of the men on Capitol Hill. At all times I tried to give him exact information of our views regardless of whether he agreed with us or not. Generally we were not very far apart.

He had one of the keenest of political minds, and he was also one of the most regular of party men. One day before the 1924 campaign he was telling me of the letters coming to him from the West saying if he expected to be re-elected, he would have to come out for the McNary-Haugen Bill. His comment was:

"Well, I am a regular Republican. I am willing to go up or down with my party."

He never dodged an issue for the purpose of courting personal favor.

I rarely asked for personal favors, or appointments. You never knew whether or not he was favorable to your suggestions. You simply had to wait for results. For instance, I was especially interested in the appointment of Harlan F. Stone, a classmate at Amherst, to the position of Attorney General. I urged the appointment upon the President many times. He even told me to talk with Stone and see how he felt about it, but apart from mere conversation I did not seem to be making much of an impression. I certainly did not know what he was going to do.

One morning Bascom Slemp, the President's secretary, called me and said, "You have just made an Attorney General, and the newspaper boys want you to tell them something about him."

That was my first knowledge of the appointment. What happened was that the President had called Stone on the telephone the night before and had asked him to come to Washington for breakfast the next morning. Mr. Stone came, and forthwith was appointed Attorney General of the United States. I was in Mr. Coolidge's office about a half hour after the new Attorney General had left to go to the Department of Justice for the administration of the oath of office, but the President, knowing very well my profound interest, never even referred to the appointment. A few days later I mentioned my surprise to Mr. Coolidge.

His only comment was, "I thought you would probably find out about it."

It was the typical Coolidge way of doing things.

An Englishman's Visit

By BEVERLEY NICHOLS

The English author Beverley Nichols has recorded some of his American observations and experiences, including this White House interview with President Coolidge, in his book *The Star-Spangled Manner*, published in London in 1928.

THE STORY opens with a squeak. It should, I know, open with a rattle of drums and a caw of eagles. (I use the word "caw," having already crossed out "screech," "clamour," and "whirr." I do not know what eagles do for you, but for me they caw, in a high, arrogant tone.)

Yes—there should be drums and eagles, and an immense Star-Spangled Banner, stirring majestically in a Washington breeze. And in the foreground I should place the massive figure of America's President, silent like the sphinx and wise as Job.

All the same, the story opens with a squeak. I can make it open in no other way. For that, at first, was the thing which most impressed me.

I am sitting in a dazzling glare of sunlight. Opposite, mercifully shaded, is the silent President. There is a hush in the room, though, from outside, one can hear the echo of many sounds—the hum of motors through bright, glittering streets, the barking of a dog with which a policeman is dallying in the White House gardens, the shuffle of footsteps in many neighbouring corridors.

A hush in the room and then—once more—that nerve-racking squeak. It penetrated my consciousness so acutely that I can even set it down in terms of music.

Now, I am going into details about this matter because I wish you to realize the precise conditions under which my reception by the first gentleman of America took place. It took place on a chair which refused to be muted. It was a chair which insisted on joining in every argument, which punctuated every witticism, and which uttered a final screech of derision when I rose to say good-bye. It was a chair which was calculated to induce an inferiority complex in even the most brazen hundred per cent American. And I firmly believe that it was a chair which President Coolidge regards with the warmest affection, as one of his most staunch allies. For nobody could get the better of him on a chair like that.

Let me tell you a story. You may regard it as a diversion, but I do not think it entirely irrelevant. Not long ago a friend of mine was summoned before Mussolini. (Things like that are mere bagatelles in the lives of my friends.) He had been told of the miles of marble pavement which it would be necessary for him to traverse, under the eye of the Duce. He had been warned of the hypnotic eye, the awesome silence, broken only by the clattering of his own heels. Therefore he shod himself in rubber, and entered the presence as stealthily as any panther. The effect upon Mussolini exceeded all his expectations. He was so impressed by this silent visitor that his arms unfolded, his steely eye was imbued with common curiosity, and he rose slowly from his seat, glaring with an irresistible fascination at the extremities of my friend, who was drifting calmly towards him.

The obvious deduction is that I should have equipped myself with an air-cushion before visiting the White House. However, I had heard nothing of this Presidential ruse. And even now, I ask myself if it was indeed a ruse. For Calvin Coolidge is not the sort of man who would deliberately make a chair squeak, although, being possessed of a dry humour, he would enjoy to the full the results of its squeaking.

It is to be assumed that the President enjoys the kingly prerogative of immunity from quotation during private interviews. It is also to be assumed that this immunity applies only to his utterances on political questions or on domestic matters which it would be impertinent for a stranger to discuss.

"Very well," you may say, "having admitted those two restrictions, you deny yourself any power of quotation whatever, for the simple reason that President Coolidge has never been known to discuss any but political questions. Literature, the arts, even a discreet recognition of the soul of man, have never gained any spoken tributes from him."

Is that so? During the first five minutes, I must admit, it seemed only too true. The silent President played up to his rôle to perfection. He asked me why I was in America. Feeling rather faint, I replied that I had come over to lecture, and supervise the production of a play. To which President Coolidge replied, in firm, round tones:

"Oh!"

There was an interval of about a minute's silence, broken only by the screech of the chair. Then, still more faintly, I said:

"The last time I was here was in President Wilson's day."

President Coolidge replied, in firm, round tones, "Oh!"

With ghastly brightness, I ventured the deep, philosophical observation that the world did not seem to have altered so very much in the interval between my two visits.

President Coolidge replied, in firm, round tones, "Oh!"

At that moment, something in me began to stir. Were we two idiots, that we should waste each other's time in this manner—I muttering inanities and he saying "Oh!"?—If I had something to tell him, then, let me tell it, or be gone. Whether it was the etiquette to take the conversation into my own control or not I did not care. I had something to tell him. It was about the young men of England.

I deliberately painted the picture black, partly because it is my honest conviction that Europe bears on its face the stamp of decay, economic and political, and partly because I wanted to see how Coolidge would respond to so extreme a statement. He responded exactly as I had expected, with wary generalizations. There were

phrases about "painful recovery," references to "economic adjust-
ment," a tactful comment on the "growth of a peace spirit."

And now at last I can come to the point. I was growing tired of
beating about the bush. I said:

"I think it must be a little hard for most Americans, not excepting
you yourself, to realize quite the extent to which the younger generation in Europe are still overshadowed by the possibility of
future wars. It hangs over them like an immense cloud. It's no use
to deny the existence of that cloud. If you take a map of Europe
and put your finger on it at random, you would find a dozen reasons
for war at any spot where your finger rested. As a result, many of
the younger men are filled with a feeling of utter futility. They
feel that they are under sentence of death, and that creative effort,
in those circumstances, is worthless. I myself think this attitude is
utterly wrong—criminal almost. But you can trace the symptoms
in every phase of European art—in the long silence of our best
poets, like Siegfried Sassoon, in the neurotic, distracted plays of
Noel Coward, in numberless artists, in the whole social life of the
community itself. If people only understood that, they would also
understand our 'decadent' young men and their 'distorted' point
of view. But they never *will* understand—"

Abruptly, I stopped. There was silence. I felt acutely self-con-
scious. Had I disgraced myself? Had I taken unpardonable liberties?
Slowly I raised my head. I looked into as kind a pair of eyes as I
ever saw.

It was then that the miracle took place. For Coolidge—the "silent"
President, the man who "never looked at a picture," the man who
"could not be bothered with writers," the "arch-Philistine," the
"hard-boiled politician," said to me:

"I think I understand, more clearly than you imagine, what you
mean."

I thanked him. That, at least, was something.

He leant forward, and continued:

"Not long ago, I happened to visit an exhibition of modern
pictures. It was held at Pittsburgh, and almost every European nation was represented—your own country, France, Germany, Italy—

the whole lot of them. And as I looked at those pictures, I felt that I could see through them, into the minds of the nations which had created them. I could see the torment out of which they had been born. If that nation's psychology was still diseased, so was its art. The traces of neurosis were unmistakable. If, on the other hand, the nation was on the road to recovery, if its people were rediscovering the happiness which they had lost, the story was told in the picture, too."

He paused, and then added, so softly that I could only just hear him:

"The only respect in which I would differ from you is that I thought I observed as much evidence of recovery as of sickness."

I was so astonished to hear these words coming from the lips of Calvin Coolidge that for a moment I thought I must be dreaming.

"Do you mean to say," I asked, "that you could trace the evidence of this unrest even in a *landscape?*"

"Yes," said Coolidge, "I think I do."

Well—after that, anything else which I could say would be bathos. I felt much as Moses must have felt after he had struck water from the rock. More than that, I felt a sense of relief at the knowledge that here was a man, in the most powerful position in the world, who was far more alive than one had realized to the problems which were agitating me and my contemporaries. And so—let us leave that room, and that squeaking chair, and that quiet, courteous man who, for once in a way, had chosen to speak.

In the Black Hills

By WILLIAM J. BULOW

A Democrat, William J. Bulow served as Governor of South Dakota from 1927 to 1931. Subsequently, he was for two terms a member of the United States Senate.

A T THE TIME I became Governor of South Dakota there was a move on to invite President Coolidge to spend his summer vacation in the Black Hills. Shortly after my inauguration Senator Peter Norbeck came to me and said that my predecessor, Governor Gunderson, had extended a formal invitation to the President, and that it would be the proper thing for me to renew the invitation.

Not so long after that, word was received that the President had accepted the invitation and was coming. We were suddenly confronted with the fact that we had invited a guest, he was coming, and we had no place to put him. There were no hotel accommodations anywhere in the Black Hills suitable for the President. The only possible place that could meet the requirements was the State Game Lodge, but the former administration had leased this establishment for the summer; the tenant had made elaborate preparations for the summer tourist trade. Luckily for us, however, the tenant was a gentleman and was ready and willing to give up his lease. . . .

One day [in June, 1927] a special train puffed into Pierre, bringing President Coolidge and his party on the way to the Game Lodge. The train was scheduled to stop at Pierre for several hours to give us

117

a chance to give the President a proper reception and welcome to our state. In company with other state officials, I went to the train to meet him. I was quite excited. In all my life I had seen but one real live President before. I had seen William McKinley when he came to South Dakota to welcome the return of our soldier boys when they came back from the Philippines.

I stepped into the President's car, and when I saw him I became more excited. No one had ever told me that the President had red hair; no one had ever described his size to me, and I thought he looked rather small in stature to be a President. I expected him to be more dignified and more important-looking.

I rode with him, in an open car, from the train to the State House, where a reception had been arranged in the governor's reception room. After he met all the state officials and citizens assembled there, we got into the automobile for the return trip to the train.

John E. Hipple, Mayor of Pierre, wanted him to see the town, and especially the city park, of which he was quite proud. We started out toward the city park. The weather was hot and dry. A good South Dakota breeze was blowing, and the air was filled with Missouri River sand and dust. As we started toward the park through a cloud of dust, the President said to me, "What are we going down here for?"

I said, "Mr. President, the Mayor arranged this trip. He wants you to see the park."

He said no more for a long time. I had never talked to a President before, and was quite embarrassed; I had decided that the proper etiquette for me was to let him do the talking, and for me only to answer his questions.

After a while he said, "How do you enforce the prohibition laws in your state?"

That one made me uneasy. No one had ever told me anything about the President's habits, and for the moment I didn't know whether he was asking a simple question or hinting for a drink. I didn't want to make any serious mistake, so I answered, "Pretty well, but not absolutely." I thought this would give him a chance to explain his position. He said nothing more for a long time.

Then, as we were driving down the main street toward the depot, through streets lined with cheering people, he said, "What is the population of Pierre?"

I answered, "About thirty-five hundred."

He said, "Well, they must be about all out."

I said, "Yes, Mr. President, these people do not see a President every day."

By this time we were back at the train. The drive had taken approximately fifteen minutes, and I have given you the entire conversation that he and I had during the entire trip.

I had many pleasant visits with Mr. Coolidge after that. He spent most of the summer in the Black Hills. . . . He was one of the most interesting men I have ever met. He had a keen sense of humor.

A few days after Mr. Coolidge got located in his summer home, Mrs. Bulow and I were spending a couple of days with the superintendent of parks in a small cottage across the creek from the Game Lodge.

One morning Colonel Starling rapped on the door of our cottage and said, "The Chief wants you and Mrs. Bulow to come over for six-o'clock dinner tonight." I told him that I intended to go fishing that day up near Sturgis and that I would not be back by six o'clock.

Colonel Starling said, "Boy, when you get an invitation from the President of the United States, that is a command."

Then he asked if the fishing was any good where I was going, and I told him that it was the finest trout fishing in the world. The colonel got quite excited, and said he would like to go along; that he could drive my car and see to it that I got back in time to dine with the President. So he and Louis Crill and I drove to Davenport Dam above Sturgis, something over fifty miles from the Game Lodge, and fished all day. We had the proverbial fisherman's luck. None of us caught a single trout. We got back to the Game Lodge just in time for dinner.

The President, also, had been fishing that day, and he had had good luck and had caught a nice mess of trout. I had never eaten a meal with a President and was a little nervous. The park superintendent realized my condition and prescribed a couple of good drinks of brandy, even though it was against the law, and he was no doctor. Mrs. Bulow and I crossed the footbridge over the creek and went over to the Game Lodge. In a little while someone announced that dinner was being served. The President took hold of Mrs. Bulow's arm, and Mrs. Coolidge took my arm and marched us out to the dining room, where the table was set for four, and where two big colored fellows were ready to wait on us.

The first course was soup. The President got the first bowl, Mrs. Bulow the second, Mrs. Coolidge the third and I got the last. This gave the President a little the start of me; and it did not take him long to finish his soup; and when he did, he pushed his bowl aside and coughed a little, and one of the waiters took his bowl and grabbed mine at the same time, and took them away. I still had about half of my soup left, but that did not seem to make any difference.

The next course was fish—trout. The serving of the trout was in the same order as the soup, and the President started right in eating his trout. When the waiter set my plate before me, on it was a fine large rainbow trout. It had a very familiar look. I thought to myself, "Where have I seen that trout before?" Suddenly I remembered that at Spearfish we had the finest trout hatchery in the world, and that I had been up there many times and looked at those trout. There were thousands of them in the ponds of that hatchery, and they were so tame that they would swim right up to you and eat ground liver or ground horse meat out of your hand. I also recalled that when the President accepted our invitation to summer in the Hills, it was up to us to provide some amusement for him.

We did not want him to go hunting and shoot our buffalo, deer or elk that roamed around the Game Lodge in our state park. Since the Black Hills streams furnished the finest trout fishing in the world, we decided that was the sport. Upon inquiry, we learned that the President had never done any trout fishing, and, that being the case, we knew that he never would be able to catch one of our Black Hills trout. Oscar Johnson was our state game-and-fish warden—the best game warden that any state ever had. He knew trout. He said we had far too many old trout in the Spearfish hatchery.

So it was arranged that he should pick a couple of deputy game wardens to help him—deputy wardens who could keep their mouths shut and who could see well on dark nights. They were to round up and sort the trout in the Spearfish hatchery, and all the fish that were fifteen years old or older were to be penned up in one pond away from the rest. Then they were to get a couple of big tank trucks and seine these aged trout out of the pond into the tanks, and, when nobody was looking, they were to haul these trout down to the state park and turn them loose in the creek by the Game Lodge. They were also to stretch a wire netting across the creek under the bridge east of the Game Lodge—so that these trout could not come right up into the lodge—and another netting under the bridge two miles down the stream.

These two miles were set aside as the special private fishing ground of the President, in which no one else was allowed to fish unless by special invitation from Mr. Coolidge. The two miles of creek became the best trout fishing in all the world. Those trout would fight and battle one another to see which could grab the President's hook first. He became the nation's foremost trout fisherman.

All this flashed through my mind when I looked at that trout on my plate in front of me. The President had his trout about half eaten before I started in on mine. The first bite I took I could plainly taste the ground liver and the ground horse meat upon which that trout had lived for years. I never did like liver or horse meat either. I had much difficulty in swallowing that first bite. In fact, I never could have swallowed it at all, except for the two good big drinks that the park superintendent had prescribed for me. I got that first bite down and then two or three more down before the President finished his. As soon as Mr. Coolidge had his fish bones picked clean, the waiter took his plate and mine at the same time.

The next course was a doggoned good, sizzling-hot beefsteak. By that time, however, I had caught onto what you had to do when you eat with the President. So I buckled right into my beefsteak and ate as fast as I could. I had my plate cleaned up a little ahead of the President. That waiter who had grabbed my soup and trout away from me did not get any of my beefsteak.

After the meal was over, we adjourned from the dining room. Mrs. Coolidge took Mrs. Bulow into a room where the two women could visit and gossip. The President took me into the reception room of the Game Lodge, where there was a big fireplace. He had had them haul in some nice dry pine logs and had had his black handy-man start a nice bright fire. In the Black Hills, the evenings and nights are always cool, and a fire felt comfortable. The President had his man move a couple of easy chairs up in front of the fireplace, and then bring him a big cigar and strike a match, so he could start smoking. The man passed the box of cigars to me, and the President asked me to have a smoke. I turned the cigar down and told Mr. Coolidge that I was raised in a home where we had a great big fireplace—that as a boy I had put in a lot of time practicing chewing tobacco and spitting on the fire. That, I was an expert at that, and with his kind permission I would take a chew and see if I had lost any of my good aim.

I had dreaded the evening. The experience that I had had with the President in riding around the city of Pierre had led me to believe he didn't talk much. I soon learned that this was a bad guess. The President started talking, and he talked most of the time. I just got in a few words now and then, whenever I happened to see an opening. I was surprised about the knowledge that Mr. Coolidge had on all kinds of subjects—especially the history of South Dakota. As the night wore on and he talked about so many different subjects, I thought about what the poet, Goldsmith, had said about the village schoolmaster: "And still the wonder grew that one small head could carry all he knew." The first thing I knew, it was approaching the hour of midnight. Time had gone fast. The President had smoked several of his big black cigars, and I had chewed up doggoned near a whole plug of chewing tobacco. It was one of the most enjoyable evenings that I ever had.

In going from the Game Lodge back to the cottage, I told Mrs. Bulow that if the President ran for re-election, I would be inclined to support him regardless of who the Democratic candidate might be. Several weeks after that, at the temporary executive office in Rapid City, the President issued his famous statement that he did "not choose to run." This released me from the commitment I had hastily made.

Mr. Coolidge stayed more than twice as long in his summer home in the Black Hills as he originally planned. He liked it in South Dakota, and the people of South Dakota liked him. At various times when I visited him at his office in Rapid City and at the Game Lodge, he requested me to make out and send him a statement of the rental for the Game Lodge. I told him that we did not expect him to pay rent for the Game Lodge. He said that Congress had ordered the White House repaired. That was being done, and he had had to move out for the summer. Congress had voted him ample funds to take care of matters while he was not living in the White House, and he wanted to pay. I never sent him a bill.

A day or two before he left, he had his secretary phone me. I happened to be in the northern part of the state a couple of hundred miles from the Game Lodge. The secretary said, "The President wants you to render him a statement for the rent due for the Game Lodge. He wants to pay before he leaves."

I answered, "You tell the President that I never yet have invited a man to dinner and then charged him fifty cents for the meal. Tell him that he is not going to get any statement from me."

After that the President took the matter up with Senator Norbeck. The Senator was much interested in the welfare of the state park. I was later informed that the President made a liberal contribution to the state-park fund.

The Man in the Portraits

By FRANK O. SALISBURY

One of the most celebrated of England's portrait artists, Frank O. Salisbury painted President and Mrs. Coolidge in December of 1928.

I HAVE HAD the good fortune to paint three American Presidents, beginning with President Coolidge. It was my first visit to Washington, a romantic experience. I had come by the night train from New York on Christmas Eve, and the crisp dawn lent enchantment to the beautiful city dominated by a dome which sets an Englishman thinking of St. Paul's. I was braced with expectancy and enthusiasm for the adventure of this visit to the White House.

The President's car came to meet me, and I was taken to the suite of rooms for visitors, where, after breakfast, the secretary came to say that the President would be ready to receive me at ten o'clock. He asked if I had brought two canvasses, and I said I always carried an extra one. It was customary, he told me, for the artist who painted the President to paint his wife also.

The usher came at the appointed time and took me down to the President. He was very kind, offering me a cigar. On my explaining that I did not smoke, he said, "Well, there is very little in these days that we can offer you," for it was during Prohibition. There was a dish of fruit on the table from which he took an apple and pared it, cutting it in two, and offering me the top half. He took me round the White House, showing me the pictures. On the first landing were two bust portraits, one of Mrs. Coolidge and one of the President, which had just been painted. They were rather caricatures, and the President explained that the artist had insisted on his saying with a snarl every few minutes, "Tiger! Tiger!" It seemed to me a wild idea, and surely the last thing in the world to express the character of Calvin Coolidge, the silent man. He introduced me to Mrs. Coolidge, whose charming personality and gracious smile had won all hearts. After this I was driven round Washington to see the city. . . .

I returned to the White House for lunch round a big circular table, and sat by Mrs. Coolidge. The President scarcely spoke to anyone at the table, but took great interest in his white collie dog, directing most of his conversation and attention to it.

At three o'clock I was summoned to be ready to leave for Sapelo Island, the country home of Mr. and Mrs. Howard Coffin. The President and Mrs. Coolidge took the first car, with four detectives on the running-board and several police on motorcycles. I came next with Colonel Starling, the secretaries, and officers following. At the Grand Station a special train was waiting, and on it were sixteen reporters and cinema men. I had an apartment to myself, and settled down to a quiet read. In the evening the President sent for me to sit with him in his parlour, and we had an interesting talk before going to bed.

The train went through Savannah on to [Brunswick,] Georgia, where we were met by Mr. and Mrs. Howard Coffin, whose yacht we boarded for Sapelo Island. We had left Washington in snow; here we were in the beautiful, semi-tropical climate of South Carolina. A lovely morning it truly was, and I very much enjoyed the cruise among the islands of the coast of Southern Georgia. The photographers were all busy when we embarked, taking every movement of the President, who was quite used to it, giving them every opportunity, facing each camera in turn.

Only a few minutes after our arrival at the beautiful villa the President said he was ready for me. I found him a splendid sitter. It was quite unnecessary for me to talk, as it was natural for him to be silent and quiet. The work proceeded well and rapidly, and on the third day I started on the portrait of Mrs. Coolidge. During her sittings the President would occasionally stroll in without saying a word to either of us and go out in the same way. When the portrait was developing he looked at it quietly and then at his wife, and said, "It is like—it is actually like you, dear!" We both laughed at this, for he seemed truly surprised that a portrait should ever be like anyone.

Everyone took a great interest in the painting, and all were enthusiastic. I worked constantly, and had very little time to see the island, except after dinner. It was remarkable to go out into the woods at nine o'clock at night without a hat or coat on, remembering that it was Christmas. The huge oak trees with festoons of moss, and the blue sea in the distance, were very beautiful, and I chose this scene as a background for Mrs. Coolidge's portrait, as it fitted the colour scheme admirably.

I painted Mr. Coolidge in a light suit. We tried a robe and a black suit, but he looked like a parson. I remarked that he looked distinguished in the light suit, and he said in measured tones, "This is a very distinguished suit." He had a great sense of dry humour.

I was never able to fathom his silence, whether his mind was actively solving some abstruse problem or whether it was a mere blank. There were five of us who sat down to meals every day, but he seldom joined in the conversation. Only once during the whole visit do I remember him talking at the table, when we were discussing a very important subject relating to the political situation, and he astonished us by joining in with a very terse sentence which summed up the situation. Beyond that we had our jokes and conversations, but he might have been deaf or absent during meal-times. After dinner he would sit in the drawing-room for coffee, and on one or two occasions entered into lengthy talks with Mr. Howard Coffin concerning conditions in the motor industry. Then he would get up quietly and go to the ballroom, where a cinema was being arranged for him, and later we would all go and sit in a row in front of the screen, just five chairs, the President sitting silently through the film. When the film was over he would get up and go to his own rooms which were next door. As I was near the door I would open it and say good night, but the silent man passed out silently.

The house was surrounded with sentinels, and wherever the President went a bevy of detectives went with him; they followed him like Mary's lamb all over the island. What surprised me was that they were all dressed in soft hats and shabby mackintoshes, which gave no dignity to the Presidential party. The officers and the secretaries, however, were all smartly dressed. Mrs. Coolidge, whenever she went for a walk on the island, also had a detective with her. I could not think who this man was just ahead of us or just behind us, until she explained that she could not even go to the draper's to buy a reel of cotton without a detective. . . .

One morning we got up at half-past three and went into the deep forests to shoot wild turkeys. We rode about seven miles by car and then walked through the thicket until we divided into three parties, keeping very quiet until dawn broke. It was a delightful experience for me to attend the awakening of nature. The first to greet the morning was the croaking frog, and then the dove, and one by one the whole aviary of the forest joined in the chorus. . . .

On our rejoining the others it appeared that no one in the party had fired a shot except the President, who, it was said, had got three turkeys. We returned home and the secretary came in to tell the President that the New York papers had been ringing up saying they must have photographs of the President shooting. Would he go out and be photographed, with the turkeys he had shot? Although he was sitting for me, he left at once, changed into shooting rig, and was photographed, and in about three-quarters of an hour came back, seeming unusually quiet and very cross. When the secretary came in soon after he said, "Of course I am not going through the whole thing again," but the secretary explained that they had the Movietone, and that the gun had failed to synchronise, or something of the sort. I was astonished and greatly amused at the trouble the President took to satisfy the clamour of the Press. It is inconceivable that anything of the sort could happen in our own country.

At the end of the week the President was anxious that I should stay and paint the portraits of our host and hostess . . . , and this I did, having very much enjoyed my stay with these delightful people on this romantic island. The visit ended pleasantly with this letter from the White House:

My dear Mr. Salisbury,

The portraits of Mrs. Coolidge and myself have come and we are much pleased with them. You have all the permission I can give to exhibit them anywhere. Please accept my thanks for all your service and care.

Yours,

Calvin Coolidge

The Broadcasting Company of America asked me at this time to broadcast a talk on ceremonial painting, and I appealed to the American people to give their artists a fair chance. Why not let their judges wear gowns and wigs, robe the President, and precede him with a mace of office and uniformed supporters? The next morning some of the papers displayed on the front page a reproduction of the King and Queen's coronation photograph with the heads of President and Mrs. Coolidge inserted in such an impish way that the crown was slightly rakish, and the headlines were: "Artist Crowns King Cal and his Queen."

By ERCOLE CARTOTTO

In addition to his portraits of the Coolidges, Ercole Cartotto painted and drew many other prominent men and women, and his work is represented in a number of the country's leading galleries.

I WENT to the White House for the first time in the fall of 1927 at the invitation of the President for the purpose, in the words of his fellow alumnus, Mr. George D. Pratt, of painting "the best portrait possible of the President for Amherst College."

The President came to the room in which I was waiting and instantly began to question me. He posed for a preliminary drawing, and he talked at the same time. For three hours, divided into two period sittings, he put me through the most uncomfortable time I had ever experienced. My procedure differed from that of other artists who had painted his portrait. He wanted to know why. He questioned me on citizenship, politics, forms of government, religious institutions. I endeavored to answer the avalanche as intelligently as possible while working. Literally "punch drunk," I was drawing the President. It did not occur to me at the moment that he was taking my measure.

At the close of my study the President sent for Mrs. Coolidge. Her coming was like a breath of fresh air. The whole atmosphere changed —and the President also. Both looked at the drawing, and the President said, "Mr. Cartotto is the first artist who did not *create* a mouth for me."

Returning to Washington later to begin the painting of the portrait, I saw Mr. Coolidge every weekday for eleven weeks, the sittings ranging from fifteen minutes to any length of time he could give me. I was usually at the White House ready to work at seven o'clock. During the morning sittings the President often dictated, sometimes on speeches, or held conferences. If he gave me any time during the afternoon, he usually sat perfectly motionless. When my work was finally done to his satisfaction, he sent me an autographed copy of my drawing of him, inscribed, "To Ercole Cartotto with great esteem, Calvin Coolidge."

It happened that while I was at work on this portrait there was some agitation, well expressed in the newspapers and elsewhere, concerning the easy access that foreign artists had to official Washington, as against the lack of recognition given to American artists.

One afternoon Mr. Coolidge entered the room in which I was working, accompanied by an American member of the diplomatic corps recently home from Europe. The President introduced me to the gentleman in this manner, "Mr. X., this is Mr. Cartotto, who has painted and drawn the best portraits of me."

The American minister, hearing my name, said to me by way of greeting, "Italian or American?"

I had started to reply, "American citizen," when President Coolidge answered for me with a single terse word, "Both."

Mr. Coolidge was aware that my career began in Boston and in New England. Something had been said about my having reversed the usual process by coming to the United States to study, rather than going to Europe, as many Americans have done. Finally, the diplomat had directed his question to a naturalized citizen and a former soldier in the United States Army.

Later Mr. Coolidge expressed himself to me a little more in detail. "If you were less considerate of the land of your birth," he said, "you probably would not care so much as you do for this country. You can serve this land better and more by bringing to it the best that you inherited."

During the following three years I was to make, besides my numerous sketches, two more paintings of him, one for his fraternity, Phi Gamma Delta, another for the State House of Vermont.

Thus I was privileged to know him gradually as the humane, friendly, deliberate, and balanced person that he was—solid as the granite of his state, and yet as gentle a human being, free from all frills and veneer, as one could meet. For example, when it was not possible for me to leave Washington for a week-end visit with my family, he sent flowers to my wife.

On one occasion in his library at Northampton, I told him that if people really knew him, it would have been impossible for him to retire. When I referred to "drafting" him, he turned with a gesture of finality toward a row of books containing his speeches.

"Those are *my* works of art," he said, with just a little humor for fear of misuse. The drudgery, the attention they required, is too leavening his seriousness. "Every word in them had to be considered much of a strain to do over again."

So Different

By BERNARD M. BARUCH

Financier, public servant, and councilor of Presidents, Bernard M. Baruch became most closely associated with Calvin Coolidge in the period after Mr. Coolidge had left the White House. In 1932, the former Chief Executive was named chairman of the National Transportation Committee. This small body, upon which Mr. Baruch and Alfred E. Smith also served, was established to investigate the condition of the country's railroads.

ALTHOUGH I had heard my beloved friend, Dwight Morrow, speak frequently of Calvin Coolidge, he did not stand out from the vast number of people in Washington. So little did I know him at first, that at a luncheon given by Mr. and Mrs. Edwin McLean, I found myself at the same table with a very quiet little man, and asked the lady sitting between us who he was. She said, "The Vice-President."

He appeared so much younger than his pictures. He was the type who would always look less than his years. He did not engage in the conversation, but he had a sly, amused look in his eyes that was in no way portrayed in his countenance.

The next time I saw him was in the White House, where I dined with him. Besides the President, Mrs. Coolidge and Mrs. Stearns were there. The President was much preoccupied, but became very companionable upon the appearance of a big collie. Addressing his remarks to the dog, he made many amusing comments on the political situation in the House and Senate.

After dinner, while I was talking to the two ladies, Mrs. Coolidge remarked that the President wanted me. I looked down the hall and saw him standing in front of the study door with a box of cigars under his arm, motioning with his head for me to join him. On entering the room, he lit the fire himself, opened his box of cigars, and asked me if I would have a "see-gar." He pronounced it rather as a Southerner or Westerner would.

I remarked that the scene in the study was very familiar to me, and pointed to a little chair that I had occupied on the extreme end of the so-called Wilson War Cabinet. He said, "You are just as welcome here now and in that chair as you were then."

The immediate warmth and friendly spirit of the man was something which I had not expected to encounter.

Then, to my utter amazement at his directness, he said, "I want to talk to you about the railroad situation."

And he did all the talking. From that topic he proceeded to the agricultural question, and the tariff, and the tax problem, which was under consideration in the Congress at the time. Although I can do my share of talking, I found that at the end of each dissertation I had to interrupt to say, "Mr. President, in order that the record may be clear as to what I think, please let me say this."

When I had stayed as long as I thought I should, I started to leave, but he wanted to talk on, and I was delighted to hear his views and to see that he was so much more human and so much more a companion than I could have believed from the stories I had heard.

And then, as I was saying good-by to him, he made a remark which perhaps explained why Mr. Coolidge had the reputation of being a silent man. He had asked me to take a certain position that I said he should reserve for some of his prima donnas who felt they should be recognized. He cackled, kind of—an evidence that he was boy and man like the rest. Evidently I had an amused look in my eyes, for he asked, "What are you smiling at?"

I said: "Mr. President, you are so different from what people say you are. My smile indicates both amusement at that and interest— and, I hope, friendliness."

He seemed to be very pleased. Then I added, "Everybody said you never say anything."

"Well, Baruch," he replied, "many times I say only 'yes' or 'no' to people. Even that is too much. It winds them up for twenty minutes more."

The next time I saw him was on a Sunday morning when he asked me to stop over on one of my trips South. He met me in the large room just off the elevator on the second floor. There was a fire in the fireplace. After discussing the matter he had in mind, the subject of disarmament came up. In the course of his remarks he went into one of those well-known Coolidge silences. He looked into the fire, took a couple of puffs on his cigar, and finally said, "If the people want to fight, they will fight with broomsticks if they cannot find anything else."

Shortly afterward he asked me to serve on the George Washington Bicentennial Commission. I went to the second meeting, a very large one, held in the Crystal Room. Numbers of people spoke about this thing and that thing. The President sat behind a little table facing the committee, which was seated in a great semicircle. After considerable time had been taken up by the speakers, and as he turned his head from one end of the semicircle to the other, he gave me an almost imperceptible wink. I was not quite certain of it at first, but each time his eyes passed mine I could see that innuendo-like wink, with just a little crinkle in the corner of his eyes. I thought it was a physical defect, but found on inquiring that this was not so. I knew then that it was mischief or something akin to it. This was confirmed some time later—how much later I do not remember—when, referring to the occasion, he said, "That meeting had *some* speakers, didn't it?"

It was only later, after he had retired from the Presidency, when we both became members of the National Transportation Committee, that I saw developed and let loose the human qualities in him that had crept out on each occasion with me. During the committee

meetings he handled everything with such rare good taste and judgment, and with so much consideration for everybody, that he won the
real affection of us all.

One day Governor Al Smith said, "Mr. President, did you know
that the rooms you are occupying now were once occupied by The
Association Against the Prohibition Amendment?"

Without batting an eye the former President said, "Well, I guess
we can fumigate them!"

The high regard in which he held Al Smith, and which Al Smith
held for him, was very pleasant to the other three on the committee.
Every meeting became an occasion we all remember. Many people
thought this sweetness and great consideration, as shown in his latter
days, were due to his approaching illness, but my contacts with him
in other matters made me believe that he always was the human
being—very shy, but always considerate of his associates.

I never heard him say anything about himself. He was entirely
impersonal, never talking about his relationship with anyone. Of
course he did have ideas about thrift and the value of money, and
what it meant to wrest a living from the hard hills where he was
born. He knew that people there had to fight for an existence and
store up for the future, as he and his forefathers had done for so
many years.

After one of the committee meetings we were discussing current
economic and social conditions in general when he said to me:
"You know, I don't understand what all this means. It is very
confusing to me."

Then I said: "Well, it is confusing to a man like me, too, because
as a boy I had to live through the Reconstruction period, when we
had a very unkind Government over us. We had to fight our way
out; and up in Vermont you had to fight your way from under very
serious economic and social difficulties. It is pretty hard for men who
had to do this to think that the Government should mother us too
much."

Before I knew him I had thought of him as a politician. As I got
to know him better I commenced to think of him as Dwight Morrow
had told me about him. He and Dwight Morrow had some similar

characteristics. The main difference was that Morrow talked, and loved to talk, and was always charming in his conversation. You loved him immediately you saw him. One admired his brilliancy, his great heart. Calvin Coolidge was shy, said nothing, but yet had all the human qualities Dwight had. That is undoubtedly the bond which held them most strongly.

It may be that my views regarding Calvin Coolidge were colored by the confidence he seemed to have in me, or perhaps it was the backing he gave to those with whom he was associated as chairman of the committee. Each letter to me made me feel I had to work harder. Here is a paragraph from a letter written in Northampton:

"It is hard for me to make decisions up here when I am out of touch with things. I thought we came to the conclusion that it was not wise for us to interpose in these emergency measures. One way is to approach this subject with entire candor and interpose wherever we think we have an opinion. Another way is to proceed more diplomatically, avoiding positions that would probably be ineffective, and looking to securing the largest result in the end."

This was in reference to my desire to get upon the statute books a bankruptcy act facilitating the quick reorganization of the railroads. After I had advocated this at one of our meetings, he made a characteristic Coolidge remark in opposition, saying, "In families where there has been a hanging, they do not like to have anybody around twirling a rope."

As an evidence of his sense of humor, I quote the following from a letter written on October 27, 1932:

"I shall go to New York on Tuesday afternoon of Election Day and could attend a meeting Wednesday morning from nine to eleven, or in the afternoon from two o'clock to nine o'clock. I mistrust that you and Governor Smith will be rather tired on Wednesday morning, at which time I shall be glad to extend to both of you my sincere sympathy."

I quote another characteristic Coolidge viewpoint as to expenditures of the committee:

"It is necessary to watch people in Washington all the time to keep them from unnecessary expenditure of money. They have lived off the national Government so long in that city that they are inclined to regard any sort of employment as a Christmas tree, and if we are not careful, they will run up a big expense bill on us. I hope you are checking them up to see what results they are getting, either by personal contact or letter."

On another occasion when the Democratic Party was at a very low ebb, he said to me, "I am so glad you are taking an interest in politics."

I told him why I was a Democrat and intended to stay one. He said he was glad because we needed a two-party system in order that one could criticize and check the other.

That Sulky, Red-headed Little Man

By MRS. DWIGHT W. MORROW

The widow of one whose career ranged impressively over the areas of law, finance, diplomacy, and statesmanship, Mrs. Dwight W. Morrow has recorded a few of her recollections of her husband's Amherst classmate Calvin Coolidge, in whose ability and promise Mr. Morrow had always maintained a strong belief and interest.

MY HUSBAND used to take delight in telling a story of his early college days at Amherst when he and Calvin Coolidge went to the same boarding house for their meals. They had found the cheapest place in town, where they paid something like $3.00 a week. Probably that was why hash was served frequently.

Whenever hash appeared, young Coolidge had a formula that he went through very gravely, never varying it and never smiling. It seems that the landlady had two pets, a dog and a cat. As her favorite dish appeared Calvin would ask, "Where is the dog?"

The dog would be called in.

Next, "Where is the cat?"

The cat would be brought in. Then and only then would Calvin help himself to hash.

When I first knew Mr. Coolidge, I must say I was not so much impressed as Dwight had led me to expect I would be. We had gone to a reunion of the Class of '95 and had been seated with Mr. and Mrs. Coolidge in the bleachers at a baseball game. It was terribly hot, and none of us could have been very comfortable. But Mr. Coolidge was particularly silent and seemed to do very little to conceal his discomfort. After the Coolidges left, I said to my husband, "I don't see how that sulky, red-headed little man ever won that pretty, charming woman."

My husband said: "Don't be too hasty, Betty. We'll hear from that man Coolidge some day."

"Yes," I replied, "we'll hear from him—but we'll hear from him through *his wife.*"

I couldn't have known then that my husband and I would both be right.

All through those early years Dwight spoke of him as having great power in reserve. While he was Governor, but before the time of the Police Strike, we were on our way through Boston, and called upon the Coolidges at the Touraine. My daughter, Anne, a little girl then, was with us.

Later, on the train to New York, there was a group of people in our drawing room, and the conversation turned to Governor Coolidge and his political future. My husband said that in his opinion, Mr. Coolidge had real Presidential possibilities. The men present disagreed emphatically—said he was too quiet and lacked all the usual political assets of cordiality and personality.

"No one would *like* him!" one of the party said.

At this point little Anne broke into the serious discussion. She held up a finger that had a bit of adhesive tape on it over a little cut. "*I* like Mr. Coolidge," she said. "He was the only one who asked about my sore finger!"

My husband, quite pleased, of course, looked at his friends and said, "There's your answer."

A good illustration of the so-called Coolidge taciturnity occurred on the *Mayflower*, the only time I was a guest on board. It had been a delightful party over the week end, with the Secretary of State and Mrs. Kellogg among the guests. At dinner I was seated at the President's left, Mrs. Kellogg at his right. Mr. Coolidge talked very little. I didn't mind. I knew his ways. I made no particular effort because I saw that he simply wasn't going to talk. Mrs. Kellogg, however, tried very definitely to overcome his quiet. I wasn't surprised that she had no success.

The next morning, knowing the President's punctiliousness, I tried my best to be on time at breakfast. My recollection is that only the President and Mrs. Coolidge were at their places.

As I opened the door, the President was saying to Mrs. Coolidge, ". . . and where are my two fair ladies?"

Mrs. Coolidge answered, "Exhausted by your conversation of last evening!"

And finally, here are two stories that might go together because they are both about costumes and what they stood for: one, a cowboy outfit, and the other, a dinner coat. These two incidents seem to show Mr. Coolidge as having been inconsistent at least once. But when his motives are understood, I believe his attitude in both cases is logical.

During a Christmas vacation when John Coolidge was at the White House, home from school, he said to his father at breakfast one morning, "I'm going out to a tea dance this afternoon. I'll be late for dinner and I won't dress."

After a moment of silence his father said, "You will remember that you are dining at the table of the President of the United States and you will present yourself at the appointed hour properly clothed."

Now of course everybody knows that when Mr. Coolidge said that, he was referring impersonally to the exalted office that he held, and not to himself.

Because he always thought in terms of the importance of his position, his friends were baffled when he permitted himself to be photographed in a cowboy uniform given to him while the summer White

House was in the Black Hills. Several people close to the President asked my husband to speak to him about it, but he declined. At last, a man or a group of men were induced to bring up the matter. They entered their protest as tactfully as possible.

"But I don't see why you object," said the President. "The people here have sent me this costume, and they wouldn't have sent it unless they expected me to put it on. Why shouldn't I have my picture taken with it on to please them?"

"It's making people laugh," said his friends.

"Well, it's good for people to laugh," said the President.

And I believe that, even supposing he did not want to wear the costume, he was really doing it out of courtesy and consideration for those who had offered him a gift.

When the President Wept

By JOHN T. LAMBERT

A former president of the White House Correspondents Association, John T. Lambert was a newspaperman whose friendship with Calvin Coolidge reached back over many years into the period of Mr. Coolidge's early activity in Massachusetts state politics.

THE DEATH of Calvin Coolidge Jr. was a great blow to his mother and his father. He was a manly, able, likable boy, full of fun. His father had said of him, "He is a Coolidge, with his mother's disposition."

I was at Madison Square Garden in New York at the time of

young Calvin's untimely death, and I feel now the shudder that passed over the Democratic National Convention when the late Senator Thomas J. Walsh made his sympathetic announcement of it. Upon my return to Washington, I visited Mr. Coolidge at the White House to express simply my sympathy for Mrs. Coolidge and himself in the bereavement that had come to them.

The President was in the Executive Offices. He was seated at the desk, across which he discussed the affairs of the nation and of the world with the officials of Government, the foreign diplomats, the financiers, industrialists, and statesmen.

"I am sorry," I said to him. "Calvin was a good boy."

He turned slowly until the back of his chair was against the desk. He faced the wide and beautiful expanse of the south lawn. Beyond it he could see the green eminence which the Washington Monument surmounts. He spoke slowly.

"You know," he said, "I sit here thinking of it, and I just can't believe it has happened." His voice trembled. He repeated, "I can't believe it has happened."

His eyes were moist. Tears filled them. They ran down his cheeks. He was not the President of the United States. He was the father, overcome by grief and by love for his boy. He wept unafraid, unashamed. The brief moments seemed to bear the age of years.

Unwilling to leave his manifestation of grief as the recollection of my visit, I said to him:

"Calvin was a cub reporter for me once. Do you remember it?"

"I think so," he answered slowly, his voice choked by emotion.

"You and Mrs. Coolidge and the boys were at the New Willard," I reminded him. "It was the afternoon of your inauguration as Vice-President.

"I said to John: 'You had a front seat at the inauguration. You saw Mr. Harding and your father, and all the diplomats with their gold braid. I want you to write just what you saw and how it impressed you.'

"John was just in the long-pants stage then, and he had other things on his mind. When I left the suite, Henry Long (he had been Mr. Coolidge's secretary) caught up with me and said, 'Young Calvin heard what you said to John, and he asked me to tell you that he would like to do it if you would like to have him.' "

At this point in my reminiscence Mr. Coolidge turned toward me. The traces of tears were leaving.

"So Calvin wrote the piece," I said. "He described the gold-braided ambassadors and—"

"I remember it," Mr. Coolidge interrupted. A smile had come where the tears had been. It was a smile of joy.

"And Calvin wrote," I said, "that he had seen Mr. Wilson leaving the White House and he thought that was 'too bad' because he had heard that Mr. Wilson was 'a fine President.' "

"He *did* write *that?*" the President asked. "That was fine. It was like him."

The President smiled broadly, a happy smile, in contemplation of the intuitive, youthful generosity of the boy who had borne his name and the name of his father.

I know as he smiled that the memory of Calvin Coolidge Jr., the manly, able, likable, *living* boy, full of fun, was with him.

Mr. Coolidge as a Speaker

By MARK SULLIVAN

Part of Frank W. Stearns' attention in his "early evaluation" of Calvin Coolidge had been directed toward an analysis of his friend's qualities as a speaker. This same subject was, when Mr. Coolidge's Presidential years had drawn to a close, assayed by other perceptive observers. A top newspaperman and careful student of the American scene through all of the Coolidge era, Mark Sullivan earned great renown for his volumes of "contemporary histories" entitled *Our Times.*

THE MYTH of Mr. Coolidge's silence is denied by the fact of his utterances. They have not been markedly less numerous, and they have been, on the whole, rather more meaningful, than those of most of his predecessors. Decidedly—most decidedly—Mr. Coolidge can talk when he chooses to.

The writer of this article has had occasion, during the last few years, to read most of the speeches of all the Presidents since Benjamin Harrison. Such a review leads to two judgments. First, that Mr. Coolidge's public utterances as a whole have been more meaty than those of any other President since Grover Cleveland. Second, that Mr. Coolidge's speeches have been much like those of Cleveland.

To this judgment there will be violent objection from partisans of Theodore Roosevelt and especially from partisans of Woodrow Wilson.

It is true that Wilson had exalted events to deal with. It is also true that some of Wilson's addresses had high quality, and that his correspondence with Germany, preceding the armistice, probably will always have a high place in the records of that kind of diplomatic exchange. But Wilson's speeches, compared with the best of* Mr. Coolidge's, had the literary defects that accompany idealism.

Idealism is necessarily vague, rather formless. In consequence, many of Wilson's speeches have what seems today an elusive and baffling abstractness. The reader does not readily "get his teeth into them." Some of Wilson's addresses, that were most applauded when he made them, read today as if he had written them according to a formula. They seem as if he had first written out a fairly plain statement of simple fact and argument. But then, one feels, he tried to ornament them, and had the effect of diluting them. . . .

Wilson loved "purple passages." Mr. Coolidge wouldn't know what that phrase means. Compared to Wilson's speeches, Mr. Coolidge's are hard granite.

This statement applies to the best of Mr. Coolidge's speeches only. He was not always at his best. Any President is so often called upon to make speeches, in addition to his normal duties, that it is impossible always for him to be his best self. It is impossible for him always to write the whole of all his speeches. President Coolidge, like President Harding and others, is called upon to make many speeches that must necessarily be perfunctory. He is asked to dedicate monuments, or otherwise is asked to say something about a local community or a local hero.

On such occasions, necessarily, a President must ask his secretary to get together the material about the man, or the community, or the subject that is to be honored. The secretary does a perfunctory job, and in consequence the resulting speech has areas of perfunctoriness. Some such explanation as this accounts for the fact that portions of a few of Mr. Coolidge's speeches have no more elevation than an article in an encyclopedia. Indeed, a few of Mr. Coolidge's speeches show evidence that his secretary leaned heavily for his material on an encyclopedic origin.

In Mr. Coolidge's speeches there has been comparatively little of this. He has been a hard-working President. So far as human limitations permitted, he has driven himself to the writing of his speeches with the same fidelity that he has given to all his tasks. When Mr. Coolidge has done this, when he has been at his best, his speeches have ranked with the best.

By JAMES E. WATSON

James E. Watson was for twelve years a Congressman from Indiana and for seventeen more a member of the United States Senate.

I HAD the pleasure of making a number of campaign speeches with Mr. Coolidge in Massachusetts when he was a candidate for Lieutenant Governor and the second time he ran for Governor, and I was greatly interested in observing his method of speech. I wanted to ascertain, if I could, how a man who spoke without the least oratorical fervor, or without in the slightest degree getting into magnetic touch with his auditors, could enlist their sympathy and convince their judgment as he did. I found out that it was what he said and not how he said it. He had an air of wisdom, an atmosphere of knowledge that led people to believe he knew exactly what he was talking about and had a solution of all public questions.

One day on the *Mayflower* he said to me:

"I am very fortunate that I came in with the radio. I can't make an engaging, rousing, or oratorical speech to a crowd as you can, and so all I can do is to stand up and talk to them in a matter-of-fact way about the issues of the campaign; but I have a good radio voice, and now I can get my messages across to them without acquainting them with my lack of oratorical ability or without making any rhetorical display in their presence."

He laughed about as heartily as I ever knew him to do over what he regarded as his singular good fortune in this respect.

A Subtle Humorist

By WILL ROGERS

During the Coolidge administration Will Rogers wrote a series of magazine articles from abroad under the title "Letters of a Self-Made Diplomat to His President." When Mr. Rogers arrived back in the United States, the President, in accordance with his customary practice regarding returning Ambassadors, invited the famous humorist to visit him at the White House. Mr. Coolidge, like other leading public figures, was often the object of Rogers' good-natured satire and burlesque. This analysis of Calvin Coolidge as a humorist was published two years after the death of the former Chief Executive.

MR. COOLIDGE had more subtle humor than almost any public man I ever met. I have often said I would like to have been hidden in his desk somewhere and just heard the little sly "digs" that he pulled on various people that never even got 'em at all.

I bet he wasted more humor on folks than almost anybody. You see most fellows notify you that they are about to pull one, or it's done with a story—"Did I ever tell you the one about the farmer at the election?" Mr. Coolidge never did that, his were pulled with not even a change of inflection, you got it, or you dident, and it dident make any difference to him.

He never did it publically, because he told me one time that it was fatal to show humor in public office, it reacted against you. How he was able to withhold it publically is more than I know, for he was a man that very quickly could detect the sham and insincerity and "hooey," but he just had to sit there and keep a straight face and think it to himself.

One of the best and "fastest" ones he pulled on me (and he pulled many). I was to lecture in Washington on one of my periodical tours (before reforming). I dropped in and wanted him to come to my little show that night, I explained to him that there was nothing to it, only me talking for two or three hours, but that I had a very fine quartet that sang. Quick as a flash without a trace of a smile, he says, "Yes, I like singing."

Now it would have been a shame if I had muffed that one. Now just imagine how many he must have pulled on old boring politicians that went right over their heads, for they are so used to having somebody give 'em warning when one is coming. He had that real old New England humor, the "no effort" and "no demonstration" kind.

He was a great fellow. I thought much of Mr. Coolidge, told a thousand little jokes and anecdotes about him, but they were all ones that brought out some little humaness in his make-up. They were all jokes on qualities which the people admired in a man. I like all public men, but I especially liked Mr. Coolidge, and Mrs. Coolidge was just about my "Public Female Favorite No. 1."

A Selection of

WIT AND WHIMSEY

CALVIN COOLIDGE, as his White House secretary once observed, had a highly "individual" sense of humor: one that is not easy to describe, and harder yet to define.

By rightful heritage and as the result of early environment, Mr. Coolidge possessed a shrewd Yankee wit of the old-fashioned, "cracker-barrel" variety. The President who during a long and oppressive Washington rainy season was asked by an exasperated United States Senator whether he supposed the rain would *ever* stop, responded exactly as might some back-country Vermont farmer sitting round the pot-bellied stove in the general store at Plymouth Notch, when he quipped, "Well, it always has!"

Endowed with a keen faculty for recognizing the ludicrous and perceiving the incongruous, he revealed his humor principally in his reaction to everyday incidents and to conditions that were an ordinary part of the life around him. Although he enjoyed hearing them, he was not given to retailing other people's jokes or anecdotes or funny sayings. His laconic observations, dry comments, and epigrammatic utterances were manifestations of his own humorous propensities, personal responses to the amusing situations and events that he identified so readily.

During the latter part of his undergraduate days at Amherst, Mr. Coolidge had achieved, rather to the surprise of his college mates, something of a reputation as a witty and effective satirist; but it was a character that he did not long cultivate: ". . . I very soon learned," he wrote in his *Autobiography* over three decades later, "that making fun of people in a public way was not a good method to secure friends, or likely to lead to much advancement. . . ." Accordingly, he had, he declared, "scrupulously avoided" such practices ever since. At another time he voiced the oft-quoted (and, one suspects, only semi-serious) lament that every time he did use his sense of humor it got him into trouble.

Nevertheless, however assiduously he might attempt to suppress his wit, it was much too strong to be stifled entirely. He could, perhaps, successfully hide it beneath a mask of seriousness and impassive manner or behind a façade of taciturnity and formal dignity, but completely eliminate it he could not; and those who experienced any degree of close association with Calvin Coolidge had frequent opportunity to witness its irrepressible bubbling forth.

It was in its expression a direct, soft-spoken, matter-of-fact humor; but at the same time precise and penetrating. Moreover, Mr. Coolidge reacted in a swift and seemingly effortless fashion, as is attested by innumerable accounts of his quick-witted conversational retorts.

His reply to the question "What part did you take in college athletics?" has long been celebrated: "I held the stakes." And of this same sort was his response when asked to indicate his hobby: "Holding office." Or, again, his answer when queried on how it was he got his exercise: "Having my picture taken," he is said to have declared.

A story is also told of the time, during his years in the Presidency, that Mr. Coolidge was out walking with Senator Spencer of Missouri. As they were returning, the Senator jocularly pointed to the White House and asked in a facetious tone, "I wonder who lives there?"

"Nobody," the President replied quietly. "They just come and go."

On a different occasion, New Jersey's Senator Frelinghuysen was a guest at the Executive Mansion. In the course of the evening, as he sat chatting with his host, he mentioned that he had had some fine Havana cigars made especially for Mr. Coolidge in Cuba, but that, unfortunately, there had been some delay in securing the lithographed bands bearing the initials "C.C." that were to go around them.

"Well, Joe," commented the President, "you know I don't smoke the bands."

Channing H. Cox, who succeeded Mr. Coolidge as Lieutenant-Governor and, later, as Governor of Massachusetts, is the source of

another anecdote, widely repeated in slightly varying forms, which
relates to the period when Coolidge was still President of the Massachusetts Senate and Cox was Speaker of the state's House of
Representatives.

A legislative session was nearing its close, and, as was the usual
practice, the two leaders were conferring to determine what matters
would be given precedence for action prior to the adjournment.
Present also was a Senator from Boston who was vigorously determined that a bill that directly affected his district should be taken
up immediately and not be carried over to a later date. In opposition
to this insistence, Mr. Coolidge kept saying, "Senator, I don't
think that's important enough in this rush hour."—"Senator, I don't
think we can do it."

Finally, indignant and angry, the legislator snapped at the Senate's
presiding officer, "You can go to hell!"

"Senator," Mr. Coolidge shot back, "I've looked up the law and
I find I don't have to."

So far as its impact upon its auditors was concerned, part at
least of the effectiveness of Calvin Coolidge's humor often lay in
its utter unexpectedness. This was especially true during the early
period following his going to Washington in 1921, a puzzling, enigmatic figure occupying what another citizen of Massachusetts, John
Adams, the Vice-Presidency's first incumbent, had bitterly called
"the most insignificant office that ever the invention of man con-
trived or his imagination conceived." Most of official Washington
then knew of Coolidge only what had appeared in the press. The
Capital had as yet had no first-hand experience with this silent,
undemonstrative man; and, from what it had read, it was hardly
prepared to find in him any very striking qualities of wit. When,
therefore, individuals began, through some personal contact or
another, to discover to their astonishment that he was in fact endowed with a very active and refreshingly distinctive sense of humor,
reports and examples of it were swiftly dispatched and circulated
throughout the city and beyond.

In accordance with Constitutional provision, the Vice-President
of the United States presides over debate in the Senate. In addition,

by long standing social tradition he acts, also, as what has been styled "the administration's official diner-out." It was with reference to this secondary Vice-Presidential function and its endless round of dinner engagements that Mr. Coolidge is quoted as having once observed, "Sometimes I don't know whether I'm having food or soda mints, I have to mix the two so often."

Mrs. Coolidge, alluding to this same period of her husband's career, has written:

"A short time after Mr. Coolidge became Vice-President he received an invitation to dinner from a resident of Washington. He called in his secretary to ask if he knew the gentleman. He did not, and the name was not listed in the *Social Register*.

" 'No conclusion can be drawn from that,' said the Vice-President. 'I have been in it myself only half an hour.' "

By the time he succeeded to the Presidency at the death of Harding in August, 1923, Calvin Coolidge had established himself as a source from which could be expected an abundant and varied supply of droll pronouncements and witty commentary.

One of the earliest of the stories to be told of his Presidential years relates to the arrival of his first White House pay check. It is customary for the Chief Executive's salary to be delivered to him in person; and to the Treasury messenger who in performing this duty handed over to Mr. Coolidge his initial wage payment, making, it is said, something of a flurry over the presentation, the new President is, in solemn acknowledgment, purported to have enjoined, "Call again."

Remarks like these, which from another might have seemed only mildly amusing or even commonplace, were somehow, when attached to this dour, decorous Yankee in the context of his bland outward appearance, rollickingly, hilariously funny to all who heard them, either first- or second-hand.

Many of the observations and statements attributed to Calvin Coolidge were, of course, made up of whole cloth, and others, manifestly, were embroidered upon to a generous degree. Over the years countless anecdotes and bon mots have been ascribed to him which should in reality be associated with others or which, alternatively, are entirely products of clever and active imaginations. Yet so characteristic and plausible have some of them seemed—so genuine in ring and so Coolidgean in tone—that many have been erroneously accepted as authentic. Accordingly, the great body of Coolidge lore necessarily contains much that is pure fiction—or, at best, highly fictionalized.

Illustrative of this, Claude M. Fuess, Mr. Coolidge's principal biographer, tells of an investigation he pursued in an attempt to trace down the origin of the protest, "They hired the money, didn't they?" which is so frequently quoted as having been made by the President over a proposal to cancel the war debts of European countries.

"I have tried in vain," declares Doctor Fuess, "to ascertain the source of this quotation and must, under the circumstances, regard it as belonging to the Coolidge apocrypha."

With respect to this same quotation, Mrs. Coolidge has commented, in an observation she seems to have adopted as rather a standard answer to many of the queries that came to her about the authenticity of sundry remarks supposed to have been made by her husband, "I don't know whether he said it, but it is just what he might have said."

On another occasion, she wrote, "Among the stories which might reasonably be attributed to him but which did not originate with him, there is the one about sin which I have heard repeated many times. It is such a good story that it is almost a pity to refute it.

"According to the story, the President had returned from attending church service on a Sabbath morning when I had remained at home. I inquired what the sermon had been about, and his reply was, 'Sin.' Then my question, 'What did the minister say about it?' and the reply, 'He was agin it.'

"The telling never fails to bring forth a hearty laugh, and I happened to be present the first time that the President heard it. He laughed mildly and remarked that it would be funnier if it were true."

At times Mr. Coolidge's humor took a somewhat satiric turn. In this connection, Charles E. Crane has recorded an anecdote told to him by Reuben F. Wells, an Amherst fraternity brother of "Cooley's" and at one period an amateur market gardener in Hatfield, Massachusetts, near Northampton:

"The college and fraternity link led Wells to seek out the Coolidges as customers, and for a long time he served them regularly with the product of his hennery. . . .

"Wells kept but few mature hens. They were mostly pullets, and the eggs ran small. But Mrs. Coolidge never raised objection, and paid the price. There came, however, the day of reckoning.

"Wells made an occasional practice of stopping at the law office to see Mr. Coolidge. These visits were not very lively affairs, but they had Amherst college chat in common. On one particularly quiet day Wells had dropped in, and talked or tried to talk, but Mr. Coolidge seemed to have something on his mind. Finally, Wells and the future President walked out to the street together, and when they reached open air Mr. Coolidge broke the spell.

" 'By the way, Reuben,' he said, in his characteristic drawl, 'what do you keep in your henhouse? Robins?'

"It was enough said. Wells saw that the Coolidges thereafter had the pick of his biggest eggs."

John Lambert, a well-known journalist of the '20's and a friend of the President's, has provided another example of Mr. Coolidge's wit in its sardonic vein:

"A feminine guest at a White House luncheon had obviously sought this opportunity to belabor her pet enemy. This enemy happened to be an American ambassador who was understood by the Administration to have performed meritorious service. But, according to the lady's estimate, he was rough, uncouth, uncultured, and lacking in respect for the customs, traditions, and ceremonials of the ancient court to which he had been assigned.

"Tige, the old black cat that is almost a White House tradition, had sauntered into the room and was lazily rubbing itself against the table leg. The President turned to the person upon his right and said in a voice that was quite audible to the shrewish woman upon his left, 'This is the third time that cat has stopped at this table.' "

Mrs. Raymond Clapper in her *Washington Tapestry* tells of the White House caller who asked the President if he was acquainted with a certain government official.

"A very interesting situation there," said Mr. Coolidge by way of reply. "He wants to go to London as ambassador. He spent half an hour telling me considerations that should win the appointment."

"I'm sure you were aware of the many considerations in his favor before," suggested the visitor.

"Yes," said the President, tartly. "Less now."

And the story is also told of an attempt made by Ruth Hanna McCormick to secure a federal judgeship for a prominent Chicagoan of Polish descent. As a part of her campaign of persuasion, Mrs. McCormick arranged for a group of Chicago Poles to call on the President at the White House.

The delegation on being ushered into the President's office stood in stony silence, which the Chief Executive, his eyes fixed intently upon the floor, apparently had no strong inclination to break. After the passage of what seemed an eternity, Mr. Coolidge observed, "Mighty fine carpet there."

With relief and expectation the visitors smilingly nodded their concurrence.

"New one—cost a lot of money," he confided.

To this the Poles smiled even more expansively.

"She wore out the old one, trying to get you a judge," said the President, abruptly bringing the interview to its close.

It has been reported by various observers that the President seemed to care little whether his humor registered with others— whether they "got" his jokes or "caught" his humorous allusions. This was undoubtedly due to the fact that fundamentally he regarded his observations and remarks as being for his own diversion and humorous self-indulgence, not primarily intended to entertain or titillate others.

He did not expect that his kind of humor would elicit loud and hearty laughter. A smile, a grin, or just an amused glance was enough to record suitably an appreciation, and such a response usually pleased Mr. Coolidge. Yet none of these was really necessary, for the expression of wit, in and of itself, seemed to be for him both end and reward enough without any other person's acknowledgment or applause.

Mrs. Coolidge once indicated that she herself believed her husband's dry humor was, indeed, employed in large part merely for his own amusement:

"I know that is true," she reminisced, "of one characteristic comment which I heard him make, and it was uttered in so low a tone that I almost missed it.

"Across the street from us lived a Smith College professor who had been a missionary in Palestine for nine years before he came to Smith. He had many interesting stories to tell of his experiences there. My mother was always a wonderful listener. One Sunday afternoon we were all sitting on the front porch when the professor came across the street to pay us a neighborly call. Finding an eager listener in Mother, he was soon launched upon one of his favorite topics. After a while Mr. Coolidge quietly withdrew into the house. The neighbor talked on until twilight.

"After supper, when the family was seated around the evening lamp, Mother had much to say of Professor Grant and his talk about Palestine. From behind his paper I heard my husband mumble, 'He's used to talking to the heathen.' "

The famous comedian Mack Sennett considered Mr. Coolidge an expert practitioner of the fine art of "dead-pan" humor—the most difficult type of all, requiring not only a true comic gift but, also, a highly developed sense of timing.

The President would sometimes respond with rapid-fire speed, as to the effusive lady who on being introduced to him gushed the intelligence that she came from Boston: "Yes, and you'll never get over it," he declared. At other times, however, he would effectively use a "long-pause" technique, as on an occasion reported by Colonel Starling of the Secret Service detail at the White House:

". . . Jimmy Reynolds, former treasurer of the Republican National Committee, was elected vice-president of a Washington bank. He came to see the President and told him all about his good fortune, sitting on the edge of a chair in the Executive Office while the little fellow sat with his feet on the desk, slowly puffing at a cigar.

" 'Mr. President,' Jimmy said, 'you know the success I had in securing funds for the Republican party. I did not ask for any recognition or thanks at the time and I do not ask for any now. But it would do me an enormous amount of good and be a feather in my cap if you would become a depositor in my bank. Will you do it?'

"The President continued to puff at his cigar, watching the toe-tips of his shoes as he tapped them together. Finally, after several minutes of silence, he said:

" 'Couldn't you make me an honorary depositor?' "

A great many jokes and stories about Calvin Coolidge center upon his taciturnity. Naturally, the President was not without an awareness of their currency nor of the public's image of himself as decidedly a Sphinx-like character, impassive and uncommunicative; and on a number of occasions he is even known to have contributed to the "Silent Cal" legend with whimsical observations of his own:

"Has it been warm out in Minnesota?" he asked Senator and Mrs. Shipstead, who were his guests at the White House one summer evening.

"Very warm indeed," was the reply. "How has it been here, Mr. President?"

"Well, it has been hot here," the President said. "I was sitting here the other night with a lady who fainted. Don't know whether it was the weather or the conversation."

From William Allen White comes this anecdote of the same general sort:

"He sent a telegraphic invitation for Mrs. White and me to join him and Mrs. Coolidge on a party on the Presidential yacht *Mayflower* [in December, 1924]. . . . My first experience with the President came on the wharf as we embarked. The camera men wanted a picture of the party. One photographer—a moving-picture man—hustled us around for a silent news reel and then cried:

" 'Look pleasant, and for Heaven's sake say something—anything; good morning or howdy do!'

"To which Calvin Coolidge remarked dryly as he assumed his stage face:

" 'That man gets more conversation out of me than all Congress.' "

Another story told by Channing Cox relates to a time when Governor Cox visited the President in the Executive Offices in Washington. Impressed by the tidy appearance of Mr. Coolidge's desk he expressed a certain surprise:

"With all the people you have to see . . . ," Cox exclaimed, "and all the communications you have, you don't seem to be pressed for time at all. Now, back home in Massachusetts, I'm trying to fight all the time to get ahead, get ahead, and get through, so I can do some *real* work."

To this complaint on his friend's part that so much of his time at the State House was taken up in merely seeing people the President responded, "Channing, the trouble is you talk back to them."

Whimsey was decidedly a prominent element in the Coolidge humor. It was whimsey, mixed perhaps with offended frugality, that during the early days of his marriage caused him to write on the flyleaf of a household "medical companion" his unwary young wife had purchased from a door-to-door book agent, the anonymous inscription, "This work suggests no cure for a sucker."

It was whimsey, too, as well as his perverse Yankee appetite for teasing, that impelled him to suggest one day to a White House luncheon guest who had declined a cigar because he was, he said, unable to hold one in his false teeth, that the gentleman consider having a little wire platform constructed to attach to his chin in order to support a perfecto.

Everett Sanders, who was secretary to the President from 1925 to 1929, has told of having seen constant displays of Mr. Coolidge's humor arising out of their daily contacts and the transaction of routine White House business:

"John G. Sargent, then Attorney General of the United States, was a friend of very long standing, both men having been reared in Vermont—almost boyhood chums, although the Attorney General was older than the President. They spoke the same language. But to Mr. Sargent, Mr. Coolidge was the President of the United States, and he treated him with great respect and deference, and was almost timid about calling on him. He rarely came without an engagement, and always protested that the engagement was not important enough to bother the President unless he were free. The President, of course, knew this.

"One day, after calling up and being told to come right over, the Attorney General came in before the President had been told of his expected visit. I walked in to the President's desk, stood for a moment, and when he looked up I said:

" 'Mr. President, the Attorney General has just arrived.'

"He interrupted with just the hint of a smile and said, 'I suppose he is clamoring to get in.'

"To those who knew the Attorney General and knew of his deference, the supposed picture of his 'clamoring to get in' was a side-splitting joke. . . . "

Mr. Sanders reports, also, on an occasion when a large delegation arrived to be photographed with the President in the south grounds of the White House. Although they had been definitely told in advance that Mr. Coolidge would not address them, the head of the organization, just before it was time for the party to assemble, enthusiastically commented, "I am delighted to learn that the President is to make us a little speech."

"I replied very firmly," Sanders declared, "that he had been misinformed—that he was to join them for a photograph, but would not say anything. I went in and explained to the President how many times I had told them he could not make a speech, so that if they called on him he would understand.

"As he started to join them, the President said to me, with a smile: 'If they have not understood, I will elaborate on what you have said by saying nothing.' "

At yet another time, Sanders sent something to the President's attention, together with a note which read, "The attached correspondence was returned to me for filing. Would it not be well for me to send copy of this letter to Senator _____ to allay his fears?"

When it came back, he found scribbled below: "No, let him tremble."

Richard L. Jervis, a former chief of the White House Secret

Service detail, characterized Calvin Coolidge as having possessed "the greatest sense of humor" of any of the seven Chief Executives under whom he had served, from Theodore to Franklin Roosevelt.

As but one example of Mr. Coolidge's distinct fondness for pranks, Jervis has told of the time that the President first discovered, on returning from an early morning walk, an alarm button that was located on the front porch of the Executive Mansion.

"Feigning he was tired," the Secret Service aide reported, "he leaned against the button and pressed it.

"His solemn, immobile expression unchanged, he walked hurriedly into the house and from behind the safety of the living-room curtains peeked out and saw two policemen come tearing across the lawn, survey the scene, and, finding no one, return to the guard house.

"He pushed the button two more times and each time he would, without change of expression, watch the excitement that resulted."

John Coolidge once wrote of his father that he "occasionally enjoyed teasing people who did not know or understand him, and who thought that he was always very dignified. This resulted in their completely misinterpreting his efforts to be amusing, which, of course, was just what he wanted.

"One such incident occurred in a railroad dining car. The colored waiter, knowing who Father was, hovered around his table continuously and was solicitous almost to the point of being obnoxious.

"Finally he asked if everything was satisfactory.

"Father swiftly replied, 'What did you think was wrong?'

"This was such an unexpected answer that the waiter, mumbling and blinking, backed away completely nonplused."

Alfred E. Smith came to know Mr. Coolidge quite well in his post-Presidential years, and it was then that the two men served together on a small committee set up to dispose of a multimillion-dollar estate by distributing it to worthy charitable organizations.

"In the course of our deliberations," Governor Smith later made known, "a Jewish home for children was proposed as one of the beneficiaries. The man who was representing it, appearing before our committee, said to me:

" 'By the way, Governor, you know So-and-So—he's deeply interested in the home. You know him well—you play poker with him.'

"Without smiling or even looking up, Mr. Coolidge asked, 'Is that why he needs the money?' "

Smith has also recalled an earlier anecdote of the time he and Mrs. Smith were visiting President and Mrs. Coolidge during the summer of 1926 at Lake Osgood in the Adirondacks:

"While the four of us were out in a motor boat, the President and I got to talking about waterways, and I told him I would like to sell the Erie Canal to the Federal Government. It was costing New York State a lot of money, but it would be a good buy for the Federal Government as part of a ship canal from the Great Lakes to tidewater. Mr. Coolidge said he had heard some talk about the project.

"After a while our conversation got around to the measures we had been taking in the state to assure an adequate water supply to the vast, growing population of New York City. I pointed out that some day the state would be faced by a serious problem in supplying water to the people of New York.

"The President looked at me with a twinkle in his eye and said, 'Why don't you sell *them* the Erie Canal?' "

With reference to a famous anecdote known in several slightly varying texts, Mrs. Coolidge, writing some months after her husband's death, recorded:

"There is one dinner story which has been repeated more generally than any other, perhaps. I verified it myself only recently.

"Seated next to Mr. Coolidge at the table one evening was a young woman of wide social experience in Washington circles. She opened the conversation by taking him into her confidence with, 'I have made a bet, Mr. President, which I hope you will help me to win.'

"No response.

"Nothing daunted, she continued, 'It is that I will engage you in conversation for at least five minutes.'

"Raising his eyebrows slightly, but not looking in her direction, he contributed to her defeat with two words, 'You lose.' "

Even in his retirement Mr. Coolidge continued to be the source of witty remarks and amusing observations that spread all across the land. There is, for example, the answer he is said to have given to a lady who spoke to him following his address in Madison Square Garden in the Hoover-Roosevelt campaign of 1932.

"I enjoyed it so much," his admirer declared, "that I stood up all the time."

"So did I," replied the ex-President.

The famous theatrical figure Otis Skinner has preserved another story of that same election year:

Mr. and Mrs. Coolidge had come over from Plymouth Notch to lunch with the Skinners at nearby Woodstock, Vermont. "Oh, Mr. Coolidge," Mrs. Skinner exclaimed in discussing the forthcoming Presidential contest, "I wish it were you that we were to vote for in November! It would be the end of this horrible depression."

A twinkle came into the eye of the former Chief Executive. "It would be the beginning of mine," he said.

Life was a serious business to Calvin Coolidge. He was anything but a creature of frivolity and caprice. He believed in hard work, in the dedication of oneself to performing the tasks at hand, in the faithful fulfilment of one's responsibilities and obligations. Yet, at the same time, in sharp contrast to this, as well as in seeming contradiction of the outward appearances of his character and manner, he was also endowed with a keen and active sense of humor, a sprightly wit, a deep-seated whimsicality of spirit. If he was sobered by the seriousness of man's mortal mission, clearly he was quietly amused too by certain of man's frailties and imperfections, by the absurdities and incongruities of the life he saw spread about him and of which he himself was part.

That this amusement found frequent, irrepressible expression is documented by many accounts that have become a lively part of the Coolidge legend, revealing a man that despite his imperturbable qualities and stern façade, had a distinct and delightful vein of laconic humor. And Mr. Coolidge emerges, as he has been characterized by one who was close to him throughout his Presidency, a figure "half owl, half elf."

III

IN RETIREMENT

Our Neighbors the Coolidges

By F. W. PLUMMER

F. W. Plummer and his family occupied the other half of the Northampton duplex in which Mr. and Mrs. Coolidge made their home
over so many years and to which they returned upon leaving the
White House. Later, in 1930, at the time this account by Dr. Plummer
was first published, the Coolidges moved from their old Massasoit Street
quarters to a larger home, "The Beeches," in a different section of
the city.

TWELVE YEARS AGO when I moved my family to Northampton to take the principalship of the high school, I was fortunate
in finding a comfortable place to live in a part of what has been
called a duplex house. It was No. 19 Massasoit Street.

When we engaged the house we did not know who our neighbors
were to be. Later we discovered that the other side of the house was
occupied by a Mr. Coolidge, then the Lieutenant Governor of Massachusetts. We had not even known that the Lieutenant-Governor
lived in Northampton. . . .

We had originally made arrangements, through the superintendent of schools, to take another house. But he sent word that the
Massasoit Street house was vacant and that it was better and cheaper,
the last a consideration to a schoolmaster. The rent was $28 a month
then. It is now $40 a month. . . .

We have found it a very comfortable house, quite as large as the
usual single house on Massasoit Street. Each family was as independ-
ent in its arrangement as though as much expanse of lawn separated
us as divided me from my neighbor on the other side. Even the
cellars and heating systems were separate.

We each had our own front porch and back steps. The front porch is an important detail of a house in a New England town on a street like Massasoit Street. Our front porches sit a little closer to the street than most of the houses near us. The steps cannot be more than eighteen or twenty feet from the sidewalk. But that has never prevented us, any more than it has prevented Mr. Coolidge, from sitting out on the porch after supper summer evenings.

A large tree—a pin oak—affords pleasant shade to both our porches. We have never had many mosquitoes and neither our porch nor the Coolidges' has ever been screened. Mr. Coolidge is an inveterate front-porch sitter. He always was, and now that he is back home from Washington he sits out and smokes his cigar on the porch of an evening or a Sunday afternoon, and all the tourists in America shall not keep him from it.

It has been my fortune to live in several New England cities. My neighbors have been well-to-do or prosperous business and professional men. Northampton and Massasoit Street do not differ essentially from the others except in having a greater amount of cordiality and a less amount of interest in the private concerns of other families.

Mr. Coolidge knows how to mind his own business and, I believe, he has never had cause to complain of the idle curiosity of his neighbors. He was tired after the Presidency and wanted to settle down to the enjoyment of home life after the exacting demands of eight years in which he had to keep constantly alert in the consideration of many matters affecting our domestic and foreign policies. His neighbors have not been responsible for the general interest of the public which has prevented the realization of his hopes.

Hundreds of automobiles from every state pass the house every day. Sitting on my porch, I have counted the cars passing the house. Even now—just last Sunday—it is almost a procession, though Mr. Coolidge has been out of the Presidency for more than a year. Cars average one every six seconds. Many drivers pause long enough to take a few pictures. If the family is not visible, frequently whole families of tourists and sightseers pose on the steps or in front of the house while some member of the party takes pictures to show their friends at home. Often Mr. and Mrs. Coolidge are asked to pose. I do not believe such requests are ever refused. However, posing for a picture is quite a different matter from engaging in conversation.

Living in the house with such a noted personage has had its drawbacks. Hundreds of representatives of newspapers and press associations have tried to get members of my family to give interviews and to answer hundreds of questions concerning the intimate home life of the Coolidges. We have uniformly refused to give any information of any sort.

Occasionally, even now, someone rings our bell and asks if I am Mr. Coolidge. How anyone who has seen Mr. Coolidge's pictures could honor me by making such a mistake is inconceivable. Certainly the resemblance is not marked. But even some of the visiting dignitaries who attended the ceremonies notifying Mr. Coolidge of his nomination as Vice-President rang my bell and greeted me as Mr. Coolidge, announcing that they had come to pay their respects before the ceremonies.

People, evidently foreign, will ring my bell and demand, "Coolidge live here?" Others ring to ask if I suppose that Mr. Coolidge would object to their photographing the house.

Anything Mr. Coolidge does is of interest to the public. Upon the slightest excuse a score of camera, motion picture and newspaper men seem to spring out of nowhere and get ready for action in front of No. 21. Even when it was rather important for me to get down town, I have had to remain in the house or leave by the side door to avoid the possibility of getting into a picture where I did not belong.

Our lawn has been worn out by the feet of Coolidge admirers. Whenever the Coolidges were expected home from Washington the street was always closed to traffic. There would be the inevitable jam around the house. For an hour or two before their expected arrival, after the 4th of March last year, a crowd filled the sidewalk, street and front lawn, waiting. Massasoit Street will seem strange for a time, when it no longer attracts a crowd.

Moving [this fall] into a $40,000 house from a $40-a-month rental will involve for Mr. Coolidge even a greater change than those figures suggest. The nine acres and sixteen rooms at "The Beeches" will inevitably call for a material increase in the domestic personnel of his establishment. As they would say in Vermont, he will have to have more hired help. Ever since he returned from Washington they have managed with a housekeeper, who has had a part-time assistant, and one man who drives his car, tends his furnace and does other work about the yard.

My neighbor is now to have the relative seclusion of a nine-acre estate in place of his unscreened front porch. But for protection he hardly needs this. Mr. Coolidge has always carried his screen and his board fence in his own personality.

I grew up in a rural community of New England that must have provided essentially the same background as Mr. Coolidge's boyhood home in Plymouth, Vermont. I think I know the pure Yankee strain. But Mr. Coolidge is by far the most reticent man I have ever met. I don't suppose I have had a total of an hour's conversation with him in my whole residence next door. Of course, he has been away most of the time. And part of this lack of contact is a neighbor's reluctance to intrude upon a man so much beset as Mr. Coolidge. His other neighbors share that reluctance. Being the next-door neighbor of a President on a small-town side street imposes its own restrictions. Mr. Coolidge's neighbors share his own respect for the quality of minding one's own business.

But Mr. Coolidge's temperament is the chief bar to knowing him. I never heard anyone call him "Cal." I cannot conceive of anyone so calling him, any more than I can conceive of anyone slapping him on the back. His dignity would not permit it. And he never steps down from his dignity. In my twelve years next door, I have never seen him in his shirtsleeves.

Mr. Coolidge seems to resent talk. I do not mean that he is not always cordial to meet. He will always nod and speak, when he is sitting on his porch, to a passing neighbor. But it would take a very persistent acquaintance to follow up these single-sentence exchanges with words enough to make a conversation. To be sure, he will often say more than a passing on the sidewalk requires. But if to the essential "How do you do, Mr. Plummer," he adds: "Going to be hot," I feel that I have had a talk with Mr. Coolidge.

I think that anyone who has occasion to hold a longer talk than that with Mr. Coolidge must inevitably leave with the feeling that Mr. Coolidge was relieved when the session ended. You get an impression that he values your room more than your company. Yet he seems not to mind people if they don't talk. I know that in the days when Northampton saw more of him, he used often to drop in and sit for an hour at a time with a former neighbor without saying a word, just sitting and smoking and presumably pondering and enjoying himself by being with his friends. . . .

So far as a neighbor can see, ten years of the highest public office have not changed Mr. Coolidge in any particular. The only difference in his outward aspect is that he smokes cigars now in an ivory holder as he sits out on the front porch after supper. And he has a man drive him down to the office—the same man who tends his furnace and trims the lawn. Giving up his walk to the office is a step that he was driven to by his present prominence, to avoid being exploited on the street by persons with something to advertise or some ax to grind. Otherwise, he has not changed the old regularity of his habits —going to his office about eight, returning to his home for luncheon and then going back in the afternoon to close his office and be home by six o'clock.

He rigorously protects the privacy of his home. He expressed his indignation when reporters called at his house one Sunday after he had maintained office hours six days in the week. But when he learned that the cause of their visit was the death of his old friend, Ambassador Herrick, he quickly responded. Going into the house he presently returned with a typewritten statement of tribute to Mr. Herrick.

The same reporters who had been rebuked for invading his Sunday seclusion were invited in to have two pieces of birthday cake when they called on the Fourth of July for news of his observance of what is always a double celebration in the Coolidge home.

Mr. Coolidge was always well groomed. I noticed no great difference in his appearance since he has been called the best dressed of Presidents. Now, to be sure, he always looks as though he had a valet, though he depends on the public presser, as the rest of us do. Mrs.

Plummer sometimes comments how well-pressed Mr. Coolidge always is, because I tend to be a little careless in such particulars. I suppose every woman would like to see her husband as fastidious in matters of dress as is Mr. Coolidge.

I am a Democrat and come from an unbroken line of Democrats. My father and grandfather would not have dreamed of splitting their ticket or ever casting other than straight party votes. But I cast my Democratic vote for Mr. Coolidge. In this I suppose—indeed the election figures show it—I was one of millions. I suppose my reasons for casting my normally Democratic vote for Mr. Coolidge are essentially the same reasons that actuated some millions of ordinary voters —I had, of course, the additional desire to do all I could to help to the Presidency a Northampton man and a next-door neighbor. And I was not unaffected by local pride. Of course, I did not know the Democratic candidate as I knew Mr. Coolidge. But, aside from these local reasons, I knew Mr. Coolidge to be fully qualified and equipped by training and capacity for the office. I had confidence in him as a shrewd man who could not be taken in by politicians.

To me Mr. Coolidge personified the homely qualities that make possible such a pleasant, comfortable neighborhood as ours on Massasoit Street, such stability and security of family relations, and of citizenship as make the snug foundation for such happy communities to live in as Northampton is. I found a glow of satisfaction in feeling that the man who had lived in the very house with me, in rooms of the same identical size and shape, who paid the same rent and trod the same sidewalk and had his home ties amongst the same people, was to fill the greatest elective office in the world.

But I suppose nobody in Northampton thinks of Mr. Coolidge as a very great man. I do not, even though I did cast my usually Democratic vote for him. But even if he were a much greater man, Northampton would hardly measure him so. Folks are not much given to hero worship in a New England town. . . . [Yet] if the people of Northampton seem unappreciative of having a former President of the United States as a fellow townsman, this appearance is on the surface only. They are proud of Mr. Coolidge and of the distinction he has brought to this city. None of us meets him without a feeling of personal congratulation.

[Now that he is moving to a larger house] Massasoit Street is going to miss seeing this quiet man as he walks slowly along the street with his hands behind his back, apparently deep in thought. We are going to miss the sprightly step of Mrs. Coolidge as she takes her dogs out for their daily exercise. Massasoit Street will be changed. The thousands of motor cars will no longer pass our doors, but will be diverted to another part of the city. We shall have to accustom ourselves to the former quietness of a side street.

His Law Partner Looks Back

By RALPH W. HEMENWAY

In this account, written after the ex-President's death, Ralph W. Hemenway recalls some of the incidents and events of what proved to be a short-lived legal partnership but a long-continuing association of friendship. When Mr. Coolidge returned from Washington in 1929, he continued to make his headquarters at the old Coolidge and Hemenway law offices in Northampton's Masonic Block.

BETTER SIT DOWN, Mr. Hemenway. Then if he has to shoot, he'll hit me and not you."

It was President Coolidge talking. The words sound like a speech from a melodrama, I know, but they were only his way of making me feel at home in the White House on the old terms of our association in Northampton. I had gone to Washington with some legal papers for his signature. Ushered into the Executive Offices, I presented myself before him at his desk and observed the courtesies by standing without speaking before the President spoke. When he referred to somebody shooting, I was startled for only a moment. His playful meaning was immediately clear when I noticed that an armed guard was pacing back and forth at the rear of the building outside the windows.

I do not wish to convey the impression that Mr. Coolidge and I were habituated to constant joking. Life was extremely real and earnest to him, and there was nothing of the hail-fellow-well-met about him. In an association extending over eighteen years I was always "Mr. Hemenway" to him—never "Ralph" or even "Hemenway." It is, of course, less remarkable that I should have addressed him always as "Mr. Coolidge." . . .

Our business relationship was entirely impersonal in that strangely contradictory way which assumes an unspoken bond of considerable intimacy. For example, Mr. Coolidge and I were law partners for many years, and as in all partnerships, papers were drawn setting down the terms of our agreement. But the papers were never signed. They had no validity whatever—except that best validity of all by which a man's word is truly as good as his bond.

In the summer of 1915, Mr. Coolidge invited me to come into his office. I told him that I would not consider going in with him except as a partner of the firm. Mr. Coolidge replied, "Draw the papers."

I wrote an agreement whereby the split in profits was to be so much during the first two years, with an equal division beginning the third year. Later Mr. Coolidge said to me, "If I ever become Governor, the business is yours."

About four years were to elapse before his election as Governor in 1919. Thereupon he remembered just what he had said to me four years previously, and his financial interest in the office ceased.

When he was nominated for the Vice-Presidency, he asked me what I thought of it.

"With your luck," I told him jestingly, but more prophetically than I could have guessed, "I wouldn't want to be in the President's shoes for anything in the world!"

He recalled this afterward with that amazing memory of his for even the merest trifles. In fact it is his memory, his absolute integrity, and his peculiar way of doing things that remain outstandingly with me.

While he was President, I had a note in longhand from him one day, as follows:

Sept. 13, 1928

My Dear Mr. Hemenway:—

You have at Hampton safety deposit 2 Lib Bonds $50 each. See if any are due Sept 15 current and if so have Tr. Co. collect them and credit my acct.

Yours
Calvin Coolidge

That note shows his far-reaching recollection of detail. Here you witness the President of the United States, the problems of a nation on his desk, with an income of $75,000 a year and $25,000 more for traveling expenses and entertainment, plucking out of his innumerable mental pigeonholes the relatively insignificant matter of two $50 Liberty bonds on which the interest of $2.12 was due!

To show his kind-heartedness and his liberality I recall one occasion when I was in need of funds owing to the closing of a local bank. I was seated at my desk deeply buried in thoughts that were not particularly cheerful when he came through the connecting doorway from his office, walked over to me, and placed a slip of paper on my blotter. As he turned away and went back to his room, he said quietly, "And as much more as you want."

It was a check for $5000.

The splendor and pomp of Washington and of the Presidency never changed his early valuations of life. He was simple and unaffected to the last degree. He liked foot comfort. In the old days he would slip off his shoes and put both stockinged feet in his wastebasket where they wouldn't be seen. Once, however, he was taken off guard. A woman client came into his office while his feet were planted in the wastebasket. He got a good laugh out of it afterward—although he certainly did not enjoy the surprise at the moment.

Much has been said about Mr. Coolidge's sense of humor. To my thinking no man has a complete sense of humor unless he can laugh at himself. He was quite capable of that. One day after he had returned to private life he came to the office to find that Miss Hayes, who helped with his secretarial work, had not yet arrived. A head cold had caused her lateness, and when she came in, she was startled to see someone in front of the safe fumbling with the combination dial. It was Mr. Coolidge. Somewhat flustered, Miss Hayes wrote out the combination and offered it to him at arm's length—Mr. Coolidge being very careful about contracting a cold. Consulting the numbers on the paper from time to time, he went on fumbling for what seemed an eternity to Miss Hayes. At last, when her desire to help could be restrained no longer, she offered to open the safe. Taking the slip of paper and reading it, she saw to her embarrassment that in her haste she had omitted one of the numbers. No one could have opened that safe with her figures. On top of her lateness and her error she made a confused apology, not knowing what the reprimand would be. Mr. Coolidge merely looked at her and broke into a long chuckle. A practical joker himself, at last somebody—even though unintentionally—had played a practical joke on him. He could appreciate it.

Of course we ran into occasional difficulties with crank visitors at the office, but it was never necessary to have any kind of official guard for the ex-President. Once a man in a kind of naval uniform announced that he had some "imports" for Mr. Coolidge. Because of his dress and complacent manner he got by. I never saw anybody leave any place faster—with Mr. Coolidge in a towering rage behind him. He was a bootlegger, and his "imports" were liquor.

Mr. Coolidge wasn't altogether happy after his return to North-hampton from Washington. He had not intended to have an office, but almost at once his mail alone indicated that he would need some place away from home. The syndicated articles that he wrote became a trial to him in several ways, and such demands as his party made upon him and that he felt he owed to it, together with the darkening economic conditions, contributed, I believe, very materially to his untimely death.

But his humor was unfailing. One time a very gracious, well-dressed woman called—quite obviously a person of excellent background—and asked to see him. I told her that Mr. Coolidge was too busy to be disturbed, but she was extremely insistent, and I offered to take a message to the former President. From appearing entirely normal at first, the caller said excitedly that she intended to ask from Mr. Coolidge the protection of Secret Service men. I saw that I had a problem on my hands. Her voice by this time was loud enough to be heard throughout the offices. I said what I could to calm her, trying at the same time to ease her out. As I maneuvered toward the door, I hit upon what I thought would end the interview by saying persuasively, "If I were you, I'd write to Mr. Coolidge, telling him the whole thing."

She had become comparatively quiet, but at that advice she suddenly glared at me and with slow, deadly emphasis she said loudly, "Mr. Hemenway, for two cents I'd cut your damned throat!"

When she was gone, I went back to Mr. Coolidge's office and poked my head through his door. He was smiling delightedly.

"When she said that," he chuckled, "I just wondered if you had two cents."

While President, Mr. Coolidge on two different occasions offered me a Government position in Washington, but I thanked him and refused both. I was glad that I did when he returned home and came back in the office with me again, as the close association with him during the last years of his life meant a great deal to me.

I have never had, nor do I ever expect to have, a more true and loyal friend than Calvin Coolidge.

A Secretary's View

By HERMAN BEATY

Former-newspaperman Herman Beaty reports on his year of close, daily contact with Calvin Coolidge during the period when Mr. Coolidge was largely occupied with the writing of his syndicated articles which appeared in papers throughout the country under the title "Calvin Coolidge Says."

I'M GLAD you came. I think we'll get along right well together." These words, spoken in an almost expressionless monotone and accompanied by a characteristically noncommittal handshake, inducted me into the most interesting twelve-months period of a not uneventful journalistic life. I had just been accepted by Calvin Coolidge . . . as his confidential assistant and as his secretary in retirement.

The scene was a private suite in the Hotel Vanderbilt in New York; the time *eight* o'clock of a sunny morning.

There had been no reference to duties or salary. Simply a conversation of a scant quarter-hour upon personal background and experience, of seemingly irrelevant family history and general topics of the national and international scene. Then, abruptly, the favorable decision.

I have since realized that there was other and thorough inspection prior to that meeting: a luncheon with a New York publisher; dinner with a Massachusetts philanthropist-merchant; a conference with a former member of the White House entourage.

With a flash of the dry humor which few people had opportunity to enjoy, Mr. Coolidge later permitted me to see the reports upon which he had based his selection. They were, as a whole, a painful shock to a healthy egoism. "Not brilliant but completely dependable"; "well informed but apparently objectiveless"; "an exceptional capacity for loyalty"; "no political training"—these were some of the points checked marginally in the slate-hard pencil he invariably used.

Despite the fact that I had a position at that time, his acceptance that the matter was settled, settled it for me. . . .

To have "lived" with Calvin Coolidge; to have sat with him daily in his plain office in Northampton engaged in daily talks that lasted for hours; to have traveled with him on the few brief journeys he felt he could make without sacrifice of some of his self-imposed restrictions—to New York, on brief social visits to near-by Massachusetts towns, or to the family homestead at Plymouth, Vermont; to participate, in short, in the tremendous individuality which was Calvin Coolidge, was a treasured privilege.

The routine of the typical day was fixed and unvaried. Mr. Coolidge arrived at the office at or near eight o'clock. At first I tried to put my own arrival ahead, systematically, so that I could be there first. Apparently he did the same, for when we had got it nearer to seven than to eight, he said to me:

"Been here first twenty-odd years and I guess I'll have to keep on. You needn't come until nine."

From the personal mail he would select one or two letters identifiable as from close friends, leaving the rest to be cared for by the office force. With these personal letters and the two morning papers to which he was addicted, he would retire to his desk and his cigar. After disposing of the mail weeded out for his personal reading, he turned at once to preparation of the daily editorial which comprised the only regular work he assumed during his retirement.

It was my duty to have ready for him a file of clippings from the newspapers and current magazines dealing with topics which seemed to offer themes, and a concise list of subjects previously discussed or otherwise suggested. One by one, he would take up the suggested topics and talk them over. Abruptly—sometimes in the midst of a sentence—he would turn to his desk, take up his pencil and start to write. It was infrequent that he stopped before the proposed editorial had been completed, and his accuracy in judging the space led to considerable gibing as to his economy of words among the columnists and paragraphers. These did not know that the completed text was carefully counted, not so that the writer would give no unrequited service, but in reality so that the papers paying the tolls would not have to bear what Mr. Coolidge decided would be an unnecessary expense. He also remarked once that the editors had planned for a definite space and it "might put them out" if the article ran longer.

The daily stint out of the way (he called it "chore," and regarded it as increasingly irksome as the contract period wore on, because of its interference with his already small freedom of action), Mr. Coolidge was ready to see callers—and to *talk!*

Others—and among them those of longer acquaintance—still insist that he merited the appellation of Calvin the Silent. Nothing could be further from the truth, if reference is intended to his demeanor within the protection of his private office or of his study at The Beeches. I came to recognize a certain posture—when he reclined far back in his chair, one foot resting on the half-opened second drawer of his desk, a new cigar being most meticulously clipped, then rolled between index finger and thumb preparatory to insertion in the famous paper holder—as a clear command to start a conversation. The subject was left to me: something in the daily press, some personal experience in the South—for which he had a surprisingly warm interest—would gain his attention.

He had no patience whatever with self-appointed critics of the government, and most especially with expatriates or American travelers abroad who spoke disparagingly of home institutions or officials. Even the fact that some of these were from his own college was not allowed to temper his acid judgment.

"Why, two upstarts from Amherst were in Washington before breakfast one morning to tell me how we should handle the Nicaraguan trouble!" he exploded. "I didn't waste much time on them.

Seemed to me, my information and that of the State Department was better than the information at the disposal of Amherst underclassmen.

"There's too ready a hearing abroad for Americans who make a habit of criticizing their own country."

Of foreign critics, his opinion was only slightly higher:

"They say we are not 'doing our part.' They mean we are not doing their dirty work, using our army and navy to *lick* those they don't happen to like at the moment. Why, if England, for instance, was in our position today she would 'take charge of Civilization for the benefit of Humanity' within forty-eight hours!"

His evaluation of some figures prominent in the news was terse, definite and pointed. One day a news item about New York politics was under discussion, and Mayor Jimmy Walker was mentioned.

"He has the Celtic ability," Mr. Coolidge said, "to put all his goods in the front window—and leave none in reserve; has shrewdness rather than any real ability; the kind of man who, if you wake him from a sound sleep to make a speech, is able to start right in speaking. But if you examine the speech later, you will find he has said nothing worth while."

When it was announced that James J. Davis had resigned as Secretary of Labor, Mr. Coolidge commented:

"He was an excellent Cabinet member. If I was asked who was the best in my official family, I'd have to think hard to keep from saying at once, 'Jim Davis.' His department was the most efficiently administered; that government branch will give Mr. Hoover considerable trouble when a new head is named."

About his classmate, Senator Morrow of New Jersey, whom in other ways he regarded most highly, he once made a remark that seemed to me to illuminate his own political strategy:

"An amateur in politics—thinks his constituents should be taken entirely into his confidence. Well, if he tries that, it will result in a Democrat being elected in New Jersey!"

Of Everett Sanders, who was his private secretary while he was in the White House, he spoke with warm regard:

"The best secretary any President of the United States ever had.

Lincoln had John Hay but in comparison at that time, Hay was only a callow boy from the prairies."

A statement issued by an American Senator while on a foreign tour led to this outburst:

"Always a mystery to me why, as soon as they get a public office, they must go abroad to strut! Just a craze to show themselves off and they always manage to give the wrong impression to foreigners."

. . . This country's attitude toward Russia was one of the hardest problems with which he had to deal in Washington, he said.

"I always found it difficult to arrive at a proper basis for dealing with those people. We are against autocracy, inherited sovereignty, and an established church. If we went into a country for the purpose of trade where those institutions were adhered to, we would not be expected to be called into account for our disbelief in them. It comes down in fairness to this: Russia has a right to her Soviets or whatever she wants, so long as what she wants doesn't disturb the rest of us. But to send a million dollars and a hundred agitators to China or to the United States is as much a making of war as would be the sending of an army."

He was profoundly convinced that the Soviet experiment would fail. "Communism," he once commented, "will fail because what it attempts is against human nature. No man will provide me with food and other necessities of life unless he is a gainer by it in some way."

Concerning Russia's propaganda among the youth of the country:

"Their effort to proselyte among youth will fail. It may appear to succeed for quite a time—for years, perhaps. But as these young ones mature, they will be influenced by those same age-old currents. The result will be counter-revolution unless they recognize the danger and compromise in time."

A keen student of social trends, he gave this opinion of Russian women in the tides of the new experiment:

"Another ever-present danger to them is in the women. A woman is essentially a conservative. She wants to assure to the last degree protection for her children. The Soviets may appeal to the young girl but when she comes to bear children, she will abandon the fallacy of Communism as against *their* interests. Perhaps that explains the Soviet policy of taking children into state institutions in an effort to breed out gradually the urge of mother-love."

Among a group, he was less inclined to conversation. I have seen him take an abrupt departure from a group of callers visiting him at The Beeches. "Going to take a nap," he would say, without preliminary. "Glad you came," and off he would go.

The necessity for the daily—sometimes twice-a-day—nap was one of the outward evidences of his increasing age and not-too-satisfactory condition of health. Another evidence was his desire to have someone near him. Still another was the recurring attacks of what was diagnosed as an asthmatic condition. The latter, which may have been induced by stomach trouble, made it necessary for him to keep a supply of medicinal pills always with him on his travels.

It always interested me to contrast his keenness of conversation in the privacy of his own office with his close-mouthedness in public. It must have been some strange and seldom-found *inner* reticence which made it impossible for him to "thaw out," even when he greeted his oldest friends at Plymouth.

We were seated one summer day on the small porch of the Coolidge farmhouse. There was a noisy clatter up the road but Mr. Coolidge looked straight ahead over the blue hills of the Notch. Finally a farm wagon drew abreast and the typical specimen of the rugged mountaineer of the section who was driving made an almost imperceptible movement of his whip.

"How 'ye, Cal?" he greeted.

"How 'ye, Zack?" replied Mr. Coolidge.

The wagon rattled on and disappeared around the corner. Several moments passed, and then:

"Zack Brewer. Cousin of mine. Haven't seen him—must be twenty years!"

After the daily article was written and mailed—Mr. Coolidge was punctilious about having it ready on time—opportunity was given me to view him through the eyes of his correspondents.

The Coolidge mail at Northampton was in interesting miscellany. Dozens of requests for autographs each day, in almost every case granted and supplied from cards written in advance; letters from former and current officials, here and abroad, relating to matters in which they felt he had an interest; letters from scholars and savants, asking his opinion frequently on subjects of which, he told them, he knew nothing.

In the correspondence inspired by the daily editorials were many from plain American citizens—mothers and fathers, usually, expressing their deep appreciation of the emphasis they found he placed in his writings upon the basic American ideals and virtues.

He received a surprising lot of gifts by mail—wrist watches, boxes of cigars, English lavender, books. One day an astounding thing happened. One of the packages opened contained a diamond bracelet. The woman who sent it wrote that in these times there was nobody she felt she could trust except Mr. Coolidge, and she requested him to safeguard it for her.

He treated that diamond bracelet as if it were a scorpion. He inquired carefully as to whom it was from and had it immediately packed and sent back to the sender, taking care that the post-office receipt was filed and that there were ample witnesses to its return.

Most of the letters coming to him were answered. Briefly, usually not more than a couple of lines, but an answer nevertheless. He insisted firmly that *every* communication from a church or a religious organization should have a reply, regardless of the source or the topic of the communication.

Like the mail, the daily grist of callers was a varied throng. Tourists who wanted an opportunity to sit at his desk when he was out. Coolidge enthusiasts—fanatics, some of them—who simply must see him in the flesh, regardless of the hour; the run-of-the-mill politicians, usually with an ax to be ground; distinguished visitors from abroad; and now and then such intimate friends as Frank W. Stearns from Boston, Whiting from Holyoke, Sanders from Washington, whose visits amidst the stream of those who interested him slightly, or not at all, were obviously delightful to him.

He wanted to be polite, but he was crowd-shy. One Sunday, in response to a phone call, I went up to The Beeches after church and found him waiting for me to take a stroll with him. He complained of the interest of the crowd.

"Why," he said, "I can't go down Main Street and look in the shop windows without being pestered."

He was not permitted to have even his Sunday stroll. As we reached the gates at the entrance of The Beeches, a car stopped and Mr. Average American rushed toward him. "Mr. Coolidge," he said, "I have been waiting for years—"

Mr. Coolidge turned his back on him and ran up the path to his house. He had his hands clasped at his back under the tails of his morning coat, and I shall never forget how those coat tails flirted in the face of the admirer who had disturbed his Sunday peace.

To his extreme reticence and concealment of spirit must be attributed the entirely unwarranted opinion held by many that he was "close." I have watched or assisted in the distribution of too much largess to indorse such an opinion. His code of economy can be truly translated into a desire to get his money's worth. In fact, I have myself benefited—and far beyond any fair desert—from his pathetically concealed generosity, which keenly realized any need but lacked ability to express regard or sympathy in what is considered a normal manner.

A few weeks after my arrival, Mr. Coolidge passed my desk and placed upon it a shiny, new, expensive traveling bag. Without a word, he passed on, took his seat at his desk and drew his correspondence to him. I turned around.

"For you," he said.

"But I have one."

"Too small."

Only such a code could explain the apparent contradiction of his action of wrapping, with his own hands, a Christmas package containing one hundred dollars in gold for his friend, Mr. Lucey, the Northampton shoemaker, with Mr. Coolidge's wrath when he learned that someone had been cutting wood on his "sugar lot" in Plymouth, Vermont.

I recall that he dictated at once a note to former Attorney General Sargent and asked that he proceed at once against the culprits. The fact that the stolen wood could not have been worth more than a couple of dollars, at most, or that legal abilities which quite recently had been busy with *billion*-dollar cases were being pressed into service, did not seem at all incongruous to him—or to me. The wood was *his* and something more than a mere property-right was being transgressed.

Meticulous in money matters, he kept to the end a series of small pocket memorandum books in which he entered every check received and every bill paid. From these he made up himself at his own desk his state and federal tax reports. He was his own tax expert.

He showed me, one day, the first of the series of these books which was started when he first came to Northampton as a law clerk. That year, as I recall, his income was under $250, but there was a net balance at the end of the year.

"Did better next year," he said, "and paid back my father the money he had advanced for my board."

He grumbled over household accounts like any John Smith—but invariably it was because they were not detailed to suit him, or had come to him without first being checked and approved by Mrs. Coolidge. He could tell you offhand what it had cost him to live during any one of the early years, and insisted that he could go back at any time with his family to $1,200 a year without depriving himself or them of any real comfort.

Mr. Coolidge's antipathy to waste, as well as his keen repugnance for opening himself to any situation in which someone might make capital of his name or belongings, was vividly illustrated to me one day after I had been in Northampton several months.

"Want you to go up home with me," he said, as he prepared to leave the office.

Whether by design or not, there was no one in the upper apartments of The Beeches when he led me into his own suite, and from the closets began to pull down old suits and overcoats. Still without explanation, he handed me a pair of small scissors and himself took a keen pocketknife.

"Take out any tailor marks or name tags," he said. "These are still too good to throw away, but Mrs. Coolidge says I must get rid of them. Can't let anyone resell them as mine."

After the suits had been denuded of identification marks—he carefully inspected those I had handled—I put them in my car, drove to a small town a considerable distance away and sold them to a secondhand dealer.

"Pretty good trading," was my reward when I handed over the twenty-odd dollars I had received. . . .

One thing that I learned by my sharing of his views will surprise those who concluded that the Vermont hills were his all-absorbing passion—the secret desire of Calvin Coolidge, I learned, was—to travel!

Frequently, in his office and dinner conversations, I heard him express regret that he was not "able" to go abroad for a year or more. A famous steamship line, having heard of his desire for travel, tried vainly to convince him that a completely secluded deck could be arranged for a South American tour.

The handicap was not financial, of course, and I do not think that shyness barred him. It lay in his own conviction that he could not go in a strictly private capacity; that, regardless of precaution or promise, his appearance in a foreign country would be the signal for *official* reception and ceremony. In such case, he explained each time the subject came up, it would "detract from the influence of *Washington.*" I observed that he never used the name "Mr. Hoover" in place of "Washington."

The facetious suggestion I made at the dinner table that he might get around the handicap by traveling in disguise brought an almost audible chuckle, as Mr. Coolidge tried to visualize himself in black whiskers and smoked glasses.

The inadequate substitute for travel abroad was found in his trips to Plymouth, and in one-day visits to Amherst, Springfield, Boston, and New York. Even on these trips and among a population to whom he was a familiar sight, he was annoyed by the attention he drew.

He was irked by New York traffic. One day when he was attending a directors' meeting in the financial district, a note from him was delivered to me at the Vanderbilt. It said: "Come and get me."

I called for him downtown and suggested as we left the building that we go by taxi. He hated the traffic snarls of Manhattan streets and chose, instead, to return to the hotel by the Lexington Avenue subway.

It was the rush hour. He squeezed into a seat between two stout Italian women. I stood near by, holding a strap and trying to block as many "bumpers" as possible. Suddenly one of the Italian women glanced at her neighbor and recognized the ex-President. Her glance attracted the attention of the other side of the sandwich. The way they looked at him sidewise was screamingly funny. Their interest spread to the passengers in that car and the next. But Mr. Coolidge sat looking soberly in front of him until we reached our station. He made no comment upon the ride which, I am certain, was his first in the New York "underground."

When Calvin Coolidge refused to renew his newspaper contract, there was a tremendous amount of conjecture as to his reasons. Having been given credit by the press and the public for a high regard for money, it was amazing that he should end this income, especially since virtually all the subscribing newspapers were eager that the daily article be continued.

There are several explanations for his declination. I remember one day that an intimate friend praised the series and congratulated him on the continued public interest in them. Then, in a manner that reminded me of the "I do not choose to run" episode, he said, "But I am going to stop writing them." He gave various reasons to friends who inquired why.

First, he felt that he'd covered every subject. Second, the daily task was too confining. He could not take a journey even around the state of Massachusetts without having on his mind the necessity to get the daily article written to meet closing dates. Third, the depression was being felt and he was uneasy about the immense revenue he was deriving from the writing. He said that he thought that in these days when newspapers were forced to cut down their staffs he should not be drawing so much money from them. He overlooked, of course, with his lack of newspaper experience, that the amount was made up by payments from hundreds of newspapers which were getting value received out of the series in circulation. Fourth, he knew that a national political campaign was coming on and that by the nature of the articles he would be expected to discuss candidates and politics. He had certain feelings and opinions, and a desire for impartiality, and did not want to be subjected to temptation to use his editorials to promote party interests. I think a combination of all of these was the reason this year of stimulating conversation with Calvin Coolidge came to an end.

On the day we parted, he called me by phone at my hotel from The Beeches, having already made generous provision for me.

"Mr. Beaty," he said, "I don't know that I expressed myself sufficiently at the office this morning; but—life hasn't ended for either of us."

It is this cryptic remark growing (I like to believe) out of suppressed emotion that I remember as the episode of my whole experience which came nearest to disclosing the kindly, the lovable, the *unknown* Calvin Coolidge.

I'm a private citizen now

By BRUCE BARTON

Before, during, and following his years in the White House, some of the most revealing and authoritative of the articles which were published about Calvin Coolidge were prepared by Bruce Barton, the widely-known writer and advertising executive.

THE Masonic Block of Northampton is on Main Street near the railroad station. It is a substantial brick building, four stories high. The square, old-fashioned elevator runs during the week, but not on Saturday afternoons or Sundays; and its week-day performance is deliberate enough so that the average individual with business to transact on the second floor uses the stairs. They have been well worn by many feet.

At the top of the stairs and around to the left is the glass door marked:

COOLIDGE AND HEMENWAY

Law Office

Walk In

The office was originally two rooms, but since the return from Washington of a former partner, three other rooms have been added.

Entering the principal door, you find yourself in a little outer office where Mr. Beaty, private secretary, meets and deals with the constant stream of folks who want to invite Mr. Coolidge to speak, or ask him to endorse something, or who will be satisfied if they and their aunt from Muskegon, who is eighty-nine, can just be allowed to peek in and see him at his desk—"She will remember it all the rest of her life." Beyond this are two rooms in which stenographers are typing "No" in courteous language. Next is Mr. Hemenway's office, where he sat when they started, and continued to sit while his partner went down to Washington for a while, and continues to sit now.

Separated by a thin partition from Mr. Hemenway's office is Mr. Coolidge's own room. A plain flat-top desk of shiny oak is set across one corner. On it are newspapers, reports of business statistical organizations, letters, and a few books. His chair in the corner faces some oak bookcases filled with legal volumes. On the walls are decorations such as might be found in any country law office: a steel engraving of Abraham Lincoln, facsimile copies of the Declaration of Independence, Shakespeare's will, and the warrant for the execution of King Charles I. Also a calendar from a lithographic house. To the left is a door by which an ex-President may, in an emergency, get out into the hall while his secretary is in the front office explaining and apologizing.

We passed through this door and downstairs to the same car in which Mr. Coolidge had ridden in Washington. He bought it from the Government. It is official etiquette that the President enters an automobile first, is first into the dining room, and first served at the table, taking precedence even over the First Lady. Instinctively I stepped back to let him get in, but he motioned me forward.

"I'm a private citizen now," he boasted.

We drove up Main Street. A Smith College girl out for an afternoon walk recognized him and smiled, and he returned her smile. In front of the hotel a man pointed at us, and two others turned around to stare. We swung around a couple of corners and drew up before a pair of iron gates hung between stone pillars. Each pillar bears a bronze plate: "The Beeches."

A private road connects with the street, and Mr. Coolidge owns the land on both sides.

"No policeman can tell *me* to shovel off my sidewalk," he chuckled.

The house is modern, with shingled sides, and windows divided into small panes. The doorway is attractive; there are sleeping porches at the rear. It's the kind of house you find in every suburb inhabited by people of good taste and moderate means; the kind of house a college professor would build, as a college professor did build this one. It is smaller than I had expected. The newspapers described it as having sixteen rooms, "but there are four rooms we can't find," Mr. Coolidge told me.

The lawn covers about two acres, giving space for a two-car garage and a tennis court. A fence and a tall hedge are on two sides; the other two are protected by Nature, for the land drops sharply a matter of fifty or sixty feet to the broad meadows which stretch toward the Connecticut River and Mount Tom. Somewhere down there are his boundaries; he has never been down to see just where. The whole lot is "nine acres more or less," and if a survey is ever made he has no doubt it will show that he owns what he paid for.

We walked all around, accompanied by Beauty, the white collie, and Tim, the chow. Tim lived in the White House and while he is cordial, his nose turns up a little, as much as to say, "I have been *something* in my day."

Mr. Coolidge pointed to his tall trees, and showed me the airport which can be seen from one corner of the lot, and the main road to Springfield in the distance, along which the lights were beginning to appear. He moves with a quick, springy step, almost a glide, smooth and effortless. His great-grandmother had a trace of Indian blood.

"Is it the Indian strain that makes the Coolidges so silent?" I asked.

He does not think so. His grandfather was a great talker, he said.

It was growing dark. We passed through the doorway into the front hall, which is guarded by a grandfather's clock. The library is at the right. Straight ahead is the living room, with an open fireplace. A portrait of Mrs. Coolidge hangs on one wall; she wears a dashing gown of orange-red, and the portrait is a better likeness, with more of her vivacity and charm, than any picture of her I had ever seen. Over the fireplace is an oil painting of the *Mayflower*. There is a portrait of Calvin, the boy who died, and Keller's painting of the scene in the farmhouse when Coolidge took the oath of office by the light of an oil lamp. The piano has photographs of all the family, and one of Mrs. Hoover with her first grandchild. The dining room is at the left. At the rear of the living room French doors lead out onto the sun porch, which looks toward Mount Tom.

Mr. Coolidge led the way upstairs to one of the front bedrooms, where I was to sleep. Across the hall is Mrs. Coolidge's sitting room, with her typewriter and her radio. As we entered the door she rose and came toward us, wearing a smart little green beret and a simple frock which made her look almost girlish. She had seemed tired during those last days in the White House, but now she was fresh and rested and smiling.

"It surely agrees with you to be home," I remarked. And she answered, "You just can't imagine how good it is."

We went down to the library until suppertime, which according to the tradition of the country town, was promptly at six o'clock. It was a dandy supper, with a crab-flake cocktail, and soup, and fried chicken that melted in the mouth, and watermelon pickle, with preserved pears for dessert.

After supper Mr. Coolidge and I went to the library and talked of all sorts of things. Only part of his books are there, he explained.

He has more than four thousand, and the shelves will hold only fifteen hundred. "After trying to divide four into one and a half I gave it up, and stored the others. Some day I'll have to build on an extension."

I brought up the name of Professor Charles E. Garman, of Amherst, to whom Mr. Coolidge devotes so many pages in his autobiography. I was in the last class which "Charlie" Garman taught; he died during my senior year. He seemed to us like a prophet; his words were the words of one who had spent his whole life in the contemplation of eternal truths.

On Coolidge and Dwight Morrow and every Amherst man in the nineties and early nineteen hundreds, Charlie Garman put an indelible stamp. He taught them about the laws that govern the mind. He taught them to weigh evidence, and discard the false and cling to the things which were proved. He made them believe that behind the universe there is a Plan, and that whatever true words are spoken, whatever courageous acts are performed, are not in vain.

Mr. Coolidge and I talked for a long time about Garman and how it is not necessary that a man should amass wealth or hold high position in order to exercise vast influence. Outside of Amherst, few knew that quiet, modest man, yet how many have wielded a greater power? He opened the eyes and helped to establish the thinking of hundreds of men; and one of these men became President of the United States.

For two years now he has been ex-President. He had hoped to travel and, rejoicing in their new freedom, he and Mrs. Coolidge set forth. They reached Florida safely, and had a good time. With simple faith, not supposing that anyone would be interested in an ex-President, he wrote to the postmaster in New Orleans, asking him to engage a room at the hotel and *not* to notify the newspapers. What a chance! At the depot there were five thousand crowding, struggling men and women. The two visitors looked out in terror. Before they reached the hotel they were almost torn to pieces.

From that point on there was no relief. Everywhere the train stopped were crowds and reporters and photographers. After several weeks Mr. and Mrs. Coolidge slipped back into Northampton, and they have never had the courage to leave it. Their dreams of travel are gone.

Mr. Coolidge showed me a big treatise on the Constitution bound in red morocco. He referred me to two long letters from George Washington. I read them through. The first, written to a friend who had preceded Washington to the Capital, gave detailed instructions concerning the selection of suitable living quarters. There was no White House as yet, and the first President explained carefully why he could not accept private hospitality and just what sort of place he should have in keeping with the dignity of the office.

The second letter was written when Washington was about to conclude his second term. Addressed to a friend in Philadelphia, it directed the purchase of two strong horses that could stand the trip through the mud to Mount Vernon. They must be well broken; they must be mares, so that subsequently mules might be bred from them. Most minutely the letter covered every detail of their selection and cost.

"He certainly thought things out in advance," I remarked.

Coolidge was silent a moment, and then said deliberately, "He was the only man in American public life who never made a mistake."

"I met one of your fellow insurance directors the other day who says that *you*, also, are always right," I answered.

Mrs. Coolidge had come quietly into the room and overheard the remark. "Send him up to talk to me," she laughed. . . .

Breakfast on Sunday morning was at eight o'clock, and consisted of fruit and oatmeal and sausages, and cakes with Vermont maple syrup. I asked Mr. Coolidge if he slept better in Northampton, now that the terrific burden of the Presidency was gone. He said he has always been able to sleep pretty well:

"In Washington I went to sleep quickly, but if I had a hard problem on my mind, I would wake up in the middle of the night. And the tougher the problem, the earlier I waked up. Sometimes it was hard to go to sleep again. Of course, everything a President does is subjected to criticism. But I used to remind myself that that criticism probably wouldn't bulk very large in the pages of history. And then

I would reflect that the country seemed to be in pretty sound condition. So I would roll over and go to sleep."

After breakfast he and I drove down to the post office. He came out with an armful of letters, which we took across to his office. He opened a few: Invitations to speak. Comments on his syndicated articles. Suggestions of ways in which he could save the country. More invitations to speak. He commented dryly:

"People seem to think the Presidential machinery should keep on running, even after the power has been turned off."

He added that his distaste for public functions has become almost a complex. He has served his time; he has had enough:

"If I speak, it takes a lot of preparation. If I go, and don't speak, the people are disappointed. And the other speakers all talk about me."

I mentioned his syndicated articles. "Of course, some of the smart wisecrackers take an occasional shot at them," I said.

"Yes," he smiled. "They criticize me for harping on the obvious. Perhaps some day I'll write one on *The Importance of the Obvious.* If all the folks in the United States would do the few simple things they know they ought to do, most of our big problems would take care of themselves."

We went back to the car and drove down a side street toward the railroad tracks, stopping in front of a dumpy house. It bore the sign:

FRANK FASANO

Shoe Shining Parlor

"I'll blow you to a shine," he said.

I protested. "You are blowing me to board and room and gasoline. I'll blow *you* to the shine."

But he was firm.

The door of the house was closed. Frank Fasano had not yet arrived at his place of business.

"We'll wait," said the ex-President. "He has five children. He would not like to have us go away."

In ten minutes Frank appeared. He was overflowing with thanks.

"So kind of Your Honor, Mr. Coolidge," he said. "Thank you so much for waiting, Your Honor." Mr. Coolidge said nothing. He and Frank are old friends. Frank has been shining his shoes for twenty years, ever since he was Mayor of Northampton—ever since he was "Your Honor."

We drove around the town. He showed me the Stoddard House, built by Northampton's second minister; and the campus of Smith College, where he was notified of his nomination for the Vice-Presidency. We passed the little corner house which he and Mrs. Coolidge had rented from a professor the first year of their marriage, and the famous "two-family house" where they spent so many later years. Then it was almost time for church, and we went back to The Beeches to get Mrs. Coolidge.

Nobody seemed to pay much attention as we slipped into the family pew halfway down the aisle of the Edwards Church. Just the Coolidges and a guest taking their customary place. The pastor, a nice-looking youngster in his early thirties, preached an earnest sermon against war. He had served in the Great War and he hoped his little boys would never have to serve. Out of the corner of my eye I glanced at the quiet man beside me. I wondered what thoughts were passing in his mind as he listened to the boy's plea for the abolition of armies and navies—he who had been commander-in-chief of an army and a navy.

When the benediction had been pronounced I looked around just in time to catch a glimpse of Mr. Coolidge gliding smoothly and swiftly out the door. Mrs. Coolidge and I followed more slowly, stopping to chat a moment with the preacher. Mr. Coolidge was waiting for us beside the car. People nodded in friendly fashion. We got in and were driven back to The Beeches.

After dinner Mrs. Coolidge and I talked about the younger generation. They seem good and straightforward and wholesome to her, she said. John and Florence, for example. They are good youngsters. They live in their four little rooms in New Haven, and Florence does the cooking. John likes his railroad job so much that he did not take any summer vacation. His pay is small, but they are happy. Sundays they drive up to see her parents, "and fill up their tank with father's gasoline." Yes, Mrs. Coolidge likes the young people. They are franker, perhaps, than in our day, but levelheaded, with their feet on the ground, genuine.

Mr. Coolidge came in to say that he was going up to the attic to unpack a couple more boxes of books. I went along. The attic is a billiard room with a table that was once in the old Amherst House. He may have played on it when he was a student; it looks venerable enough. Boxes and bags and trunks were all around. While he poked among the boxes, picking out the volumes that he wanted to take downstairs, I glanced at seven big scrapbooks. They were the social records of his administration, the guest lists of all the White House functions.

List after list; page after page. I looked at him across the room, bending over his boxes, fussing around like any other householder in any other attic. Perfectly contented. No more dress-suit dinners. No more hand-shaking. No further political ambitions. No regrets.

We went downstairs, and for a while we glanced at the Sunday papers without saying anything. When it was time for me to go, Mrs. Coolidge came down. They went out with me to the car and said they were glad I had come to see them and hoped I would come again. They seemed very happy as I looked back to wave them good-by from the gate. It was peaceful there under the trees, in front of their own house—just he and she, and Beauty and Tim.

IV

THE CLOSE OF
A CAREER

A Final Effort

By EVERETT SANDERS

A lawyer and former Congressman from Indiana, Everett Sanders served Calvin Coolidge in the capacity of Secretary to the President from 1925 to 1929, and from 1932 to 1934 he was Chairman of the Republican National Committee.

I KNEW . . . that his health was not what it should be. The first evidence, however, that this was a matter of concern to the former President was in a letter which I received from him last June, following my selection as Chairman of the Republican National Committee.

This and several subsequent letters and telegrams not only show the devotion of the former President to his party at a time when his health was failing, but afford a conclusive answer to those who seemed to think he should have done more in the campaign.

Though the country did not know it, he was well-nigh exhausted; and far from taking a negligible part in the campaign, these letters reveal how thoroughly Mr. Coolidge had the whole situation at heart. Considering his fatigue, they show that his efforts were little short of heroic. If I may be pardoned for introducing his personal reference to my selection as Chairman, I shall quote the first letter, which reminded me that his throat was in bad shape and that he was "having trouble about breathing."

The letter which follows was written shortly after the Chicago Convention:

June 17, 1932.

Dear Mr. Sanders:

Some time ago in discussing who ought to be Chairman of the National Committee, I said that you were the best man I could think of for the place. I am very glad that you found it possible to take it. Of course every campaign is a hard campaign and present conditions will make this a hard one, but it is going to be just as hard for the other side as it is for us. You know I should be glad to do anything I can to help. My throat, you will remember, always bothers me and it is in such shape that I do not think I could do much of anything in the way of speaking. Just at present I am having some trouble about breathing again. I am going to Vermont tomorrow for an indefinite stay, where I can be out of doors, and think I shall be all right when I get a little exercise.

I sent you the telegram because what looked like wet propaganda was being passed around to the effect that I had written an article against prohibition. I didn't know but somebody would be trying to use me as an authority and I wanted you to have the fact.

With kindest regards, I am

Very truly yours,

Calvin Coolidge

Contrary to published reports, the fact that I was Chairman of the Republican National Committee had little to do with my call on the former President at Plymouth the latter part of July. However, in addition to my desire for a visit with him, I really wanted to know from him what he could do in the campaign. I wired asking if such a visit would be entirely convenient.

I received a telegram from him quite characteristic:

JULY 28, 1932.

DELIGHTED STOP MY CAR WILL MEET YOU AT LUDLOW OR RUTLAND ANY TIME YOU SAY

CALVIN COOLIDGE

I had mentioned Ludlow and he had concluded that I had not

had the proper transportation information. He thought Rutland preferable and was putting it in my mind.

When I arrived at Rutland I was very much surprised to find that he had come to meet me. Mr. Coolidge was sitting in his automobile near the station, and his secretary came and piloted me to the car. He did not look well. To tell the truth, I was disturbed by his appearance. He was thinner and his face was paler than usual. I had seen him daily and hourly at the White House for four years, and I knew the expressions on his face and his movements almost as well as it was possible for anyone to know them.

We soon set out for Plymouth. He pointed out the landmarks on the way—the mountains and streams by name—and told me many incidents in connection with them. When we came to his home in Plymouth, with almost boyish enthusiasm he showed me over the newly remade homestead.

The carpenters were still at work remodeling the old home. The fine library and living room was unfinished, but he showed me the woodwork that was going in, the high porch on the side, the windows that would give him abundant light, the spacious arrangements that would amply take care of the extensive library which he had collected. This was to be his workshop and the source of inspiration and recreation in his declining days. He was preparing for the leisure of mind to which his years of public service had entitled him. He was at home here.

He was proud and happy with this mansion of ease without pillared posts or marble steps or official guard with golden braid. . . . In this old homestead he had taken the oath of office as President of the United States, administered by his father by the light of a coaloil lamp. It was a surrounding which furnished a perfect setting for Calvin Coolidge.

He had been called to serve his country. He had served his time. The term of enlistment was over. He knew he would not re-enlist. He was not living in the days of the past but the days of the present.

I remained for the night and until the next afternoon, and we spent a great deal of time driving among the beautiful hills of Vermont. I told him of the progress of the campaign. He was intensely interested. Despite the fact that he felt he was out of touch with politics and governmental affairs, he gave me more information about campaign plans during the day than he had during the entire four months in 1924, when I was director of the Speakers' Bureau and he the candidate for President of the United States.

I spoke to him about the part he might take in the campaign. He said he would be glad to do what he could. I later brought up the subject again, and he said he had completed an article for *The Saturday Evening Post* about the Republican Party, regarding which he had informed me previously, and asked me to read the manuscript. I asked him if he thought he could make some speeches. He said he did not know whether he would be able to make speeches during the campaign; that he was not very well—his throat was not in good shape.

In addition, Mr. Coolidge said he was rather out of touch with governmental affairs, which would make it difficult for him to develop subject matter. He then said he might make a speech over the radio, and wanted to know if I thought it could be done from his Northampton home. I said I felt sure it could.

Then I learned from him for the first time that it was intended that former-Governor Alfred E. Smith should write a corresponding article for *The Post* on behalf of the Democrats. He said he thought the Governor would come out for Franklin D. Roosevelt. I asked him whether he thought we could carry Massachusetts. He replied that if Smith supported Roosevelt vigorously and spoke in Massachusetts, it might go Democratic.

He was, however, rather optimistic at that time of Republican success. A great many small factories were resuming work, and he thought there was beginning to be a demand for manufactured products. This demand might increase in sufficient volume to start the other large factories. If that should occur, he felt we had a good chance to win.

Mr. Coolidge wanted to be left alone by the newspaper correspondents and news photographers. He was a private citizen and was no longer, as he put it, "A subject for news reels or newspapers." I had given out in New York that I was paying the former President a visit, and a sound-news-reel man came and wanted Mr. Coolidge and me to talk for him. Mr. Coolidge was considerably irritated at the request, but finally permitted him to take a still picture. This picture, reproduced later, gave evidence of the former President's illness.

On my return to Republican National Committee headquarters in Chicago, I was deluged with requests for Coolidge engagements. The newspapers had carried the story of my trip and my report that the former President would do whatever he could to help. Candidates for the Senate wired me and came to see me, urging me to get him for their states.

The importunities were so great that I wrote to Mr. Coolidge asking him if he could make a speech, perhaps in Indiana or Illinois. I was worried about both states. Although President Hoover was making tremendous inroads with powerful speeches, we all knew that he ought not to increase the number so as to interfere with their fine quality.

In response to my letters, I had a letter from Mr. Coolidge indicating that he wanted to help, but didn't believe "his throat would last ten minutes." He said:

Sept. 21, 1932.

Dear Mr. Sanders:

Your letters have been received. Everybody that has a cause wants me to make a speech about it. I have said all I know in the article which I have already prepared. If I should start to make speeches the public would expect them to be of the same character and substance as when I was in Washington. I am off here in the country where I do not have any sources of information and have purposely kept out of politics. I cannot for the life of me think of anything important to say that I did not put into the article I have already written, nor is there anyone to take care of my throat, which I do not think would last ten minutes. The last time I tried to make a speech was at Marion, Ohio. I am telling you these things to indicate that while I want to help I do not know how I can do much in the speech-making line. Do you know of anything to talk about that I did not discuss in the article I prepared?

Mr. Henry L. Stoddard wants me to make a speech in New York. I suppose no one knows how I hate making speeches.

What we need to win this election is organization. Talking is all right, but the side that organizes and gets the vote to the polls is the side that wins. Every campaign is hard, but I think we can win.

With kindest regards, I am

Very truly yours,
Calvin Coolidge

Then, as if an afterthought, and suggesting, in spite of the objections, how earnestly he desired to grant the requests, he wrote in longhand at the bottom of the letter:

"What subjects can I discuss?"

Showing how the matter weighed on his mind and that he was struggling to find a way to meet the political demands made upon him, Mr. Coolidge wrote me another letter the very next day.

Sept. 22, 1932.

Dear Mr. Sanders:

You were probably able to determine from my letter of yesterday that I am very much in the fog. I am wondering if it would not be possible for you to make a little more noise. When things are manifestly with you, it is a good idea to keep still, but when they are doubtful, as they always are in elections, some publicity in behalf of the chairman might be helpful.

I have written Mr. Stoddard to see what he has in mind about the New York speech that he wanted me to make. My knowledge of present politics is so meagre and the public would naturally expect so much from me that I am very much afraid I shall only produce a disappointment that will hurt the ticket.

I certainly hope that you will put your reliance on organization. Perhaps you can get hold of the central figures in business, industry and labor, and work down from them. I have been trying to think of something I might say, but as I have told you, I do not know of anything that I did not put in *The Saturday Evening Post* article.

With kindest regards, I am

Very truly yours,

Calvin Coolidge

I had purposely refrained from injecting my own personality into the campaign. Nevertheless, I thought well of his suggestion that "I make a little more noise" and realized the sagacity of his advice as to when it was wise to be silent in a campaign and when to be vociferous.

Had I realized the grave condition of his health, I, of course, should not have pressed him. However, it must be remembered that I had a tremendous responsibility to try to win the campaign. Accordingly, I wrote him urgently the next day:

September 23, 1932.

Dear Mr. President:

I am grateful to you for your two letters.

Since writing to you, a very great number of people have written or spoken to me about your making a speech. Senator Glenn, of Illinois, wants you to make one in Chicago, which, he said, was the only way he could be re-elected to the Senate or that Illinois could be carried for Hoover.

I think it is my duty to tell you what I think of the situation. My duty to you, my duty to the party, growing out of my accepting the responsibility as its campaign head. My duty to the country whose interests, in my opinion, are at stake. I firmly believe that if Roosevelt and Garner should go in with the heavy backwash of a number of inexperienced and radical Democratic members of Congress—with the heavy demands by veterans and other groups for treasury raids, and with no one at the White House to stop the raids, the Government credit might fail and work havoc.

I also believe that if our election is won, it has to be won from now on; it would be against us today. All my reports from Ohio westward are very bad.

Now, I think a speech from you would be a tremendous help. A speech in the Middle West preferably, or if you preferred, in Massachusetts. A speech on the radio would be of some considerable help, but if you could speak to an audience and let it be carried on the radio, that would be fine. I do not know what Stoddard has in mind, but it should be a straight Republican speech arranged through the organization so as to secure co-operation as to radio hookups—care not to conflict with some other big hookup, etc.

Now, you know full well I would not be pressing you about this to satisfy some locality or for the sake of not disappointing someone—I think it is sorely needed. I am following your advice about making a noise and strengthening organization.

With warm regards, I am

Very sincerely yours,

Everett Sanders

That I told Mr. Coolidge the latter part of September, "If our election is won, it has to be won from now on," indicates that I was not unmindful that the campaign might be going against us.

Several days previously, former-Senator Henry J. Allen, of Kansas, in charge of Republican National Committee publicity, had written to me from New York:

"We are still discussing the desirability of getting a fragment of Calvin Coolidge's wonderful article in *The Saturday Evening Post* into an electrical transcription.

"We are willing to send recording machinery to his house and put it up in his bedroom or anywhere else he will consent to have it, and let him speak fifteen minutes into it. We will give it a great audience in the country.

"You are the only man who can get him to do it. Will you move in this?"

I passed this request along to the former President, at the same time telling him of our campaign activities. He promptly replied:

September 26, 1932.

Dear Mr. Sanders:

I have your letter and note that you are making an intensive campaign, which is a good thing. Mr. Henry Stoddard is a very careful man, former editor of the Mail and Express, now connected with the New York Sun. He came all the way up here to see me Saturday and had been here once before. His address is Shippan's Point, Stamford, Connecticut. He said he should telephone to you Monday, which is today. I am writing him to make all his arrangements through Colonel Tilson as to time, etc. I am sure he will not make any conflict. I do not see how I could prepare two speeches.

I am telling Henry Allen to pick out what he would like to have fixed up for reproduction and submit it to me. It will have to be done here in Plymouth.

With kindest regards, I am

Calvin Coolidge

In connection with this letter there was a thing which, in the light of our present knowledge of his failing health, was significant. Just after the sentence, "It will have to be done here in Plymouth," evidently having in mind his physical weakness, he wrote with pen, "No movies or sound pictures."

Arrangements were made later by the Republican organization, assisted by Henry L. Stoddard, for the speech he delivered at Madison Square Garden on October eleventh. When I arrived in New York on the day he was to deliver the Madison Square Garden speech, I saw Mr. Coolidge in the morning. He said the speech he had prepared was a poor one, that he did not like it, but that it was the best he could do. I read the advance release of it and told him I thought it was good.

He was very much interested in the progress of the campaign and asked many questions about it when we were in New York.

He was not well that day—his throat was bothering him. He afterward told me he thought he was not going to be able to finish the speech. There was an enthusiastic crowd; the speech went over well and we received many fine comments on it from all over the country. It went out especially well over the radio.

The matter of his health was again sharply emphasized, first in a telegram he sent with regard to requests for additional speeches following the Madison Square Garden rally, and later on the same day in a letter. The telegram consisted of but four words.

OCTOBER 20, 1932.

UNABLE TO MAKE SPEECH

CALVIN COOLIDGE

The letter which followed explained to me that it was a physical impossibility for him to make any more speeches. He said he had not yet recovered from the effect of the Madison Square Garden speech.

I promptly wired him thanking him for the wonderful help he had already given and assuring him that I would treat his answer as final.

Toward the end of the campaign some other friends urged him to make a speech, and Charles D. Hilles, Republican National Committeeman from New York, told me on the telephone that Mr. Coolidge had expressed his willingness to make a radio speech the night before election if it should fit in with my plans.

I then communicated with Mr. Coolidge, telling him I was much pleased. I asked him how much time he desired. He wanted but fifteen minutes. He, President Hoover, Senator Capper, and others joined in a final appeal over the radio. President Hoover was in Elko, Nevada, en route to California; Senator Capper was in Shenandoah, Iowa; Mr. Coolidge was in Northampton; and the others were in Chicago. It was quite a good closing campaign program, and Mr. Coolidge's speech was exceptionally good.

I need hardly say that I especially prize this letter I received from former-President Coolidge, written in his own hand, after the election.

November 25, 1932.

Dear Mr. Sanders:

Since we did not win, the natural reaction will be to begin to blame each other for the defeat. That is no doubt going on, but I have seen nor heard no suggestion of a criticism of your conduct of the campaign. I feel sure that you will find nothing but gratitude and praise for the work you did and the sacrifices you made.

You will recall our victory with the aid of the dissatisfied in 1920, and how near it came to wrecking our party. You will see the same difficulty much enlarged after March 4 for our successors.

I want you to know how grateful I am for your public service.

Cordially,

Calvin Coolidge

Who but Mr. Coolidge would have called the campaign work "public service"?

The last letter I received from him was eight days before he was taken away. In this letter he said:

December 27, 1932.

Dear Mr. Sanders:

The interesting book that you sent me came and was an additional reason for my pleasure at Christmastime. I often think of you and shall never forget all that you have done for me.

Not the least of the reasons why I could not persuade myself to run for office again is the thought of the terrible burden it imposes on my friends. They have to make sacrifices which I can never repay.

With the Compliments of the Season, I am

Very truly yours,

Calvin Coolidge

If additional proof were needed that President Coolidge meant that he did not seek a further term when he wrote "I do not choose to run for President in 1928," or that he had no thought of seeking the office at any time in the future, this letter gives it everlastingly.

The sacrifices necessary to be made in public service were well known to him. He had been under the strain of public office for about a quarter of a century. I always thought that the compelling motive which led to the decision to retire from public life was the thought that it was after all better for the country not to have one man serve as President almost ten years. Mr. Coolidge said to me a number of times:

"This is not a one-man country."

His life has been largely one of public service. He regarded public service as a duty. Although he was a lifelong Republican, the country does not think of him as a partisan. He was first a fine American citizen and a conscientious public servant, who at no time allowed his partisanship to take precedence over his conception of his duty to his state and his nation.

Calvin Coolidge was held in high esteem by the people of every class and creed. That esteem continued after he had left the Presidency. The American people recognized in him their ideal of an American citizen.

He leaves a rich heritage to his countrymen—that of a private life and a public life, covering nearly all of his matured manhood, without a blemish.

By JOHN Q. TILSON

John Q. Tilson was a Congressman from Connecticut for twenty-one years and majority leader of the House from 1925 to 1931.

FROM the time Mr. Coolidge became President it was my custom to pay him an annual visit at Plymouth. At the time of my visit in August, 1932, I was again in charge of the Republican Speakers' Bureau for the East, so that it became my duty to see him in connection with the campaign. When asked what he was willing to undertake in the way of speaking in the campaign, he made it clear that he wished to do his part, but that he hesitated on two accounts—first, as to what would be helpful as coming from him; and second, as to the state of his health.

On the first point, he handed me an article prepared for *The Saturday Evening Post*, saying, "Please read this and tell me if you think I can helpfully say more in a speech."

After reading it I had to admit that he had covered the field somewhat fully, but I added that the people would gladly hear from his own lips even a repetition of the article.

On the point of his physical condition I was painfully surprised, for I had not known of it before, and as a consequence was quite satisfied to have him promise to deliver two addresses over the radio.

Later he was persuaded to make one speech at Madison Square Garden, and during his stay in New York on this occasion I became more fully aware that he was not in robust health.

As will be recalled, his speech there was well received, but he was not entirely pleased when the audience laughed at some of his unintentional humor. For instance, speaking of something that occurred during his Presidency, he began by saying in a most modest tone, "When I was in Washington—"

This was too much for his friendly hearers, who joined in a hearty, good-natured laugh. But he had not meant to say anything funny, and was in fact displeased over it.

By GRACE COOLIDGE

I LISTENED to that address made in Madison Square Garden as it came in over the radio, sitting in the little room back of the Plymouth store in which Mr. Coolidge was born. It seemed to me that he was in good form, although I realized that he was using his voice with care that it might hold out to the end. When he returned to Plymouth, I commented upon the clearness with which his voice had come through and upon the apparent enthusiasm of his audience. He shook his head and, referring to his phrase, "When I was in Washington," answered:

"They seemed to me to be in a strange mood. I never spoke to an audience which laughed before."

Undoubtedly Mr. Coolidge had been gradually failing in health for some time. His was not a rugged constitution, and the weight of responsibility which he had carried for many years took its toll. The death of our younger son was a severe shock, and the zest for living never was the same for him afterward. In his *Autobiography* he wrote, "When he went, the power and the glory of the Presidency went with him."

When he was tired or under unusually heavy strain, he suffered greatly from asthma. Throughout the last summer in Plymouth scarcely a night passed when he was not compelled to use a spray.

He suspected many foods of contributing to his discomfort and eliminated them from his diet list, with the result that he was insufficiently nourished. He lost weight and seemed very tired.

I was deeply concerned, but refrained from expressing anxiety, giving my attention to providing food which he could take without distress.

I no longer fit in

By HENRY L. STODDARD

Mrs. Coolidge once wrote of Henry L. Stoddard: "Mr. Stoddard was the first newspaper publisher outside of New England who became interested in Mr. Coolidge as a Presidential possibility. This was in 1920 when he owned and edited the New York *Evening Mail*. From that time he was one of Mr. Coolidge's most stanch and loyal supporters, his trusted friend."

IT IS MY PRIVILEGE to have had what probably was the last talk with Calvin Coolidge on national political topics, and to have been authorized by him at that time to make a public statement in my own way that he was no longer to be considered in connection with the Presidency or any other public office.

The interview took place at the Vanderbilt Hotel in this city on Wednesday, December 14. Mr. Coolidge had come to New York to attend the monthly meeting of the New York Life Insurance Company.

I was ill with the "flu" at my home in Stamford, Connecticut, that morning when my bedside telephone rang. I answered "Hello."

"How are you?" came back in a voice that sounded much like the voice of Mr. Coolidge, but I could not believe it was he.

"I am well," I replied. I did not want to make the usual inquiry, "Who is calling?" so in order to keep up the conversation I asked, "How are you?"

"I am very well," came the reply in a voice still more certainly the voice of Calvin Coolidge.

"Where are you?" I asked.

"I am at the Vanderbilt Hotel," was the reply.

Then I knew it really was Mr. Coolidge, as he always stopped at that hotel.

"I understand you are not well," he continued. "I am sorry. I thought we might have a visit this afternoon, but you are up in Stamford—"

"Yes, but I can be in your hotel in a couple of hours," I quickly replied.

"Don't take any risks with the 'flu,'" he urged. "Better stay home and get well."

"I don't know of anything that would help me get well more quickly than a visit with you," I replied, "and I'm going down."

"If you feel sure about yourself, all right," he said, "but take no chances. There's nothing important now. We can visit some other time."

"No," I replied, "I can be down about half past one."

"Good," said Mr. Coolidge. "I shall be back from the New York Life meeting then. We can have a talk."

Promptly at 1:30 o'clock as I entered the Vanderbilt Hotel, Mr. Coolidge's secretary, Harry Ross, met me. Together we went to the Coolidge rooms, the ex-President having preceded us.

"I am afraid you should not have come out," he said in kindly tones.

I found Mr. Coolidge in fine spirits and apparently in better health than for a long time. I had visited him twice during the summer at Plymouth, Vermont, and on both occasions his complexion plainly showed slow heart action. His rather timid, short steps as he then moved about made me feel that he realized that he had to be careful of himself.

At the Vanderbilt Hotel that afternoon, however, three weeks ago . . . , he walked freely and without hesitation, and his complexion seemed almost ruddy. As he sat down on the sofa, he drew out two cigars and said, with that quiet smile that all who knew him will always remember:

"As you don't smoke, I guess I will have to consume both of these myself.

"The election went against us much more heavily than I had anticipated," he said. "I suppose that, since it had to be, it is just as well that the Democrats have it lock, stock and barrel; but somehow I feel it is a mistake to break down the Hoover administration just as it is making progress toward national recovery. The Democrats will probably set aside the Hoover measures and try some of their own. That only means more experimenting with legislation. The big thing this country stands most in need of just now is economy. Unless Congress can bring down expenditures drastically all other measures will not count for much. Probably the people will have to find a way out themselves."

"The Democrats don't propose to pay much attention to Hoover in this session," I interrupted.

"That is not unusual," replied the ex-President. "It is no reflection on Mr. Hoover. A President on his way out is never given much consideration. That's politics. I remember that after the 1922 election, when the tide went only slightly against the Republicans, I could see a difference in the number and manner of visitors who came to the Vice-President's office the next winter. It seems to be human nature to want to be with the winner."

"Well," I said, "they're surely crowding around the winner now—even some Republicans or presumed Republicans."

"I haven't followed matters closely enough to understand just what they're aiming at," said Mr. Coolidge. "I am out of it and have kept out. I made up my mind not to embarrass President Hoover by comments on his policies, one way or the other, and I have never made any. The surest way to avoid it was to put my mind on other subjects, and I have done so. It was hard work for me to do that *Saturday Evening Post* article on President Hoover last summer just because I had not kept posted. Up in Plymouth, you know, you are pretty well out of the currents.

"I have been out of touch so long with political activities that I feel I no longer fit in with these times," continued Mr. Coolidge. "Great changes can come in four years. These socialistic notions of government are not of my day. When I was in office, tax reduction, debt reduction, tariff stability, and economy were the things to which I gave attention. We succeeded on those lines. It has always seemed to me that common sense is the real solvent for the nation's problems at all times—common sense and hard work. When I read of the new-fangled things that are now so popular, I realize that my time in public affairs is past. I wouldn't know how to handle them if I were called upon to do so.

"That is why I am through with public life forever. I shall never again hold public office. I shall always do my part to help elect Republican candidates, for I am a party man, but in no other way shall I have anything to do with political matters.

"I hear talk of nominating me for President in 1936. That cannot be. There is no way I can decline something not yet offered, but I am embarrassed by the discussion of my name. I cannot answer letters or give interviews about it, but I want to stop it before it gets too far. I authorize you now to say publicly, in your own way and in your own time, that I am no longer to be considered for any public office. I do not care to have you quote me directly, but you will know how to state it so that it will be accepted as authoritative. I do not think anything should be said until after the holidays; people will not be paying much attention to politics the next few weeks.

"We are in a new era to which I do not belong, and it would not be possible for me to adjust myself to it.

"These new ideas call for new men to develop them. That task is not for men who believe in the only kind of government I know anything about. We cannot put everything up to the Government without overburdening it. However, I do not care to be criticizing those in power. I've never been much good attacking men in public office. If they succeed, the criticism fails; if they fail, the people find it out as quickly as you can tell them."

"But, Mr. Coolidge, when this so-called New Deal fails to accomplish all that the people expect of it," I replied, "will they not turn to conservatism overwhelmingly and to you as its most conspicuous leader? Will it not be impossible for you to resist such a demand?"

"It was not in 1928," replied Mr. Coolidge, "and it will not be again. I am through with public life. You cannot state it too positively. Nothing would induce me to take office again."

"Of course, I will do as you say," I said, "but I would rather submit to you whatever I write."

"No," replied Mr. Coolidge. "You have my ideas, and you know how to state them. I authorize you to go ahead."

It was now time for the Springfield express back home. I motored with Mr. Coolidge to the Grand Central Station, and as I said good-by to him in the train shed he replied:

"Take care of that 'flu.' You never can tell what it may do to you. I hope the trip down has not done you any harm."

"All that has harmed me, Mr. Coolidge," I said, "is the decision you have made."

We shook hands heartily. Accompanied by his secretary . . . , he disappeared down the aisle toward his train—for me forever gone.

I'm all burned out

By CHARLES A. ANDREWS

Charles A. Andrews was, as he indicates in this brief reminiscence, an Amherst classmate of Mr. Coolidge's and, in later years, treasurer of the college.

MY ACQUAINTANCE with Mr. Coolidge began in the fall of 1891 when we were both freshmen at Amherst College. This acquaintance developed without interruption until his death.

During his years as President I saw him a number of times, but never for extended conversation. When he returned to Northampton, however, our association was resumed. He was a trustee of Amherst College and a member of its finance committee, and I had become its treasurer. I went frequently to him on matters of college business—to his office or to his home. He always kept me longer than the college business required and discussed public matters, giving and asking for opinion or judgment. . . .

I remember best the last time I saw him. We made a New Year's call on Mr. and Mrs. Coolidge at "The Beeches" on Sunday afternoon, four days before his death. I asked him bluntly as to his health, for I had known for a year or more that it was impaired. He replied:

"I am very comfortable because I am not doing anything of any account; but a real effort to accomplish something goes hard with me. I am too old for my years. I suppose the carrying of responsibilities as I have done takes its toll. I'm afraid I'm all burned out. But I'm very comfortable."

Two weeks before there had been a dinner of our college class at the home of one of its members in New York. I chided Mr. Coolidge for his absence. His unfailing sense of humor was aroused. He said:

"Of course I wanted to go, but it is difficult for me to go anywhere. They will not leave me alone. I have to be attended—a police squad goes with me. It's too much of an effort. You know—" and here came his grin and chuckle—"it's my past life that makes all the trouble—if I could only get rid of my past life! But that always stays with one."

Then we fell to talking of public affairs. Mr. Coolidge was plainly distressed. At the end he said:

"In other periods of depression it has always been possible to see some things which were solid and upon which you could base hope, but as I look about, I now see nothing to give ground for hope—nothing of man. But there is still religion, which is the same yesterday, today, and forever. That continues as a solid basis for hope and courage."

I have thought that Mr. Coolidge was a sicker man than he knew;

that his utter discouragement as to the state of our society—unlike the boy and man I had known for forty years—was evidence of the toll his work had exacted from him. Be that as it may, his confidence in the Divine was unshaken, and he had a faith and hope which reached beyond and above the chaos he saw on all sides.

On January 5, 1933

THE NEW YORK TIMES

WHEN ex-President Wilson died, people said with a sigh that a great intellectual light which had long been flickering had at last gone out. Different was the feeling when fourteen years ago the news came from Oyster Bay that ex-President Roosevelt had suddenly expired. Men looked at each other aghast at the thought that a powerful force, elemental and dynamic, had been taken from our public life. Still another popular sentiment is stirred by the death of ex-President Coolidge, without premonition or warning so far as the public knew. Of him the country had come to think as a possession to be enjoyed for years to come. He seemed like a permanent feature of the American scene. His removal from it is as if a deep-rooted oak at which we had become accustomed to look had suddenly been felled. . . .

Historians and biographers will long be busy with the public career of Mr. Coolidge. For a comprehensive and final judgment of it the time is not yet ripe, nor is the material complete. Personal recollections will for a time hold the field. A popular tradition has been established which it will be difficult to set right in some needed particulars. . . . But it certainly will not seem right as time passes to put too low an estimate upon the ability of Mr. Coolidge.

He was a man of unusual parts and powers. Behind his quiet

poise there was a great fund of shrewdness and also of the knowledge pertinent to his needs and ambitions. As a politician he had the sixth sense highly developed. Not by accident came his slow but sure advance from office to office until he reached the highest of all. He knew men and he knew the means necessary to bend them to his will. He was deeply versed in American political history. He understood how to fit his public words and attitudes to the prevailing mood of the country. It was frequently said that anybody could be a successful President when prosperity smiled on the land. But that was by no means the whole story with Mr. Coolidge. It is true that he avoided startling measures, and wished the people to feel that while he was in the White House they need not fear waking up in the morning to read of some tremendous sensation originating there. But some of his masterly strokes in office were conceived in the deepest kind of political sagacity. . . .

His public acts and achievements will swell the obituaries today. Some of the courageous positions which he took . . . and the phrases which he coined will be dwelt upon in fitting memory of the man called upon unexpectedly to succeed to the Presidency. That great office he never thought of as Jefferson did, as a "splendid misery." He took and bore all its heavy duties equably. Never to him did it occur to surround himself with official pomp or mystery. In his own person he illustrated the cherished American conception of a President as one who temporarily steps out from the ranks of his fellow-citizens to conduct the national government, and then is prepared to resume his place among them with no special claim upon their attention or their applause, except as he might be entitled to it by the continued display of fidelity to every duty and diligence in all the work that fell to him.

Doubtless Calvin Coolidge was of a type all his own. At the core he was pure New England. But in his sympathies and understandings he came to represent well what we like to think of as the especially American character. Now that he has fallen on sleep, his countrymen will love to recall the qualities which made him unique, though in all essential political convictions and hopes for his native land he was quite one with themselves.

A Shining Public Example

By ALFRED E. SMITH

As a member of the National Transportation Committee and also of the committee established to administer the charitable distribution of the Conrad Hubert estate, Alfred E. Smith, former Governor of New York and Democratic candidate for the Presidency in 1928, worked closely with Calvin Coolidge during Mr. Coolidge's post-Presidential years.

THE GREEN MOUNTAIN BOY has gone home. I had a great liking and respect for him. Beneath a chilly, reserved and dignified exterior, he was keen, shrewd, kindly and entirely free from side, conceit, pompousness and political hokum. We are often told politics in a republic produces only demagogues. Calvin Coolidge was a most successful and popular politician, but he had nothing of the demagogue in him.

I have heard it said that his silence was a pose, but he seemed to me as much as any man I have ever known, to be himself and to act in character.

Some said he was lucky, but that, after all, is simply another way of repeating what the Bible tells us, and what Mr. Coolidge was modest enough to understand, that the race is not always to the swift, nor the battle to the strong, but that time and chance cometh unto them all.

Mr. Coolidge belongs rather in the class of Presidents who were distinguished for character more than for heroic achievement. His great task was to restore the dignity and prestige of the Presidency when it had reached the lowest ebb in our history, and to afford, in a time of extravagance and waste, a shining public example of the simple and homely virtues which came down to him from his New England ancestors. These were no small achievements, and history will not forget them.

Calvin Coolidge was a salty, original character, an unmistakable home-grown, native, American product, and his was one of those typically American careers, which begin on the sidewalks, or on the farm, and prove to the youth of the nation that this is still the land of unbounded opportunity.

In the Green Mountain Country

By CLARENCE DAY

Clarence Day, a writer of great felicity and feeling, is best known for his three books God and My Father, Life with Father, and Life with Mother.

HE GOT UP at seven as usual, and he and his wife had breakfast together. At half past eight he went to his office in the town. His old friend and partner was already there when he entered. They were both early risers. They spoke with each other for a moment and then he went to his desk.

He was not feeling quite well. He said nothing about it. He had no idea that this was his last day of life.

There were a number of letters and other matters for him to go over and settle. He went to work methodically at them. He disliked to leave things undone. All his life he had attended to his duties, large or small, systematically. He was a sound, seasoned New Englander of sixty, and he had accomplished a lot.

By ten o'clock he had finished. He still wasn't feeling any better. He said to his secretary, "Mr. Ross, I guess we'll go to the house."

They motored back together through the streets and under the bare, spreading trees, till they came to the beeches and elms that surrounded his home. He had lived in half of a two-family house most of his life, but it had no grounds around it, and when he was fifty-eight he had moved; "so the doggies can have a place to play," he had said.

His wife was out—she had gone downtown on foot to do some shopping. He and his secretary went to the library. He toyed with a jigsaw puzzle a moment. They spoke of the partridge hunting they had had in October, and of the hay fever that had bothered him in July—a "pollen attack" he called it. He made little of it. He had been lucky—he had had very few illnesses.

As they sat there talking he said he was thirsty. The cook and maid were at hand, and so was Mr. Ross, but he didn't like to be waited on—he went to the kitchen and got a glass of water himself. He heard the gardener in the cellar and he went down there to say something to him. The gardener was the last man he spoke to. When people asked him later what his employer had said he couldn't remember. He told them that it was something about the house or the grounds, and that it had not seemed important—to him.

Leaving the gardener this man went upstairs to his bedroom. He took off his coat and waistcoat to shave, but sank to the floor. He was dead.

The news spread through the town. Children on their way home from school stopped to look through the gates. A few policemen arrived. When reporters and camera men came the Chief of Police took them aside and asked them not to bother the family. He left one policeman on guard and every one else went away.

The flag on the schoolhouse had been lowered. Now, on all public buildings, other flags went to half-mast. In town after town, and city after city, the flags fluttered down.

The next day the guns began booming. For thousands of miles throughout the nation, and at its army posts overseas, at half-hour intervals all day long, cannon by cannon they spoke. And when evening came and the bugles had sounded retreat, there were last, long, slow salutes everywhere of forty-eight guns, one for each of the forty-eight states of his country.

The hotel in Northampton was crowded that night. Friends of his had arrived for the funeral, and there were many reporters. The reporters swapped stories of the days before he had retired. One time when he had been suddenly needed, they said, for some national conference, and when nobody knew where he was, he had been found down in the storeroom, fishing a pickle out of a jar with two fingers. He had liked homemade pickles and people had sent him quantities of them, but he never got any at table, they were all kept on shelves in the storeroom, because of the chance that cranks might send jars that were poisoned.

Early in the morning the long special trains came rolling in. The President and his wife, the Vice-President, the Chief Justice, several Cabinet members, and committees of Senators and Congressmen got out of the sleeping cars from Washington and walked through the crowd at the station. Governors of nearby states and other officials arrived in their motors. They went to the Congregational Church and sat in its plain oak pews.

The service was brief. There was no eulogy, no address of any kind. Two hymns were sung, parts of the Bible were read, and the young minister prayed. He rose, and gave the great of the land who stood before him his blessing. They filed slowly out.

The streets emptied as the visitors left. The motors and trains rolled away.

When the town was alone with its own again, six sober-faced policemen lifted the coffin and carried it out to the street. Light rain was falling. Drops glistened on the coffin as it was placed in the hearse. A few motors fell in behind it, and the little procession moved off along the old country roads.

In every village they went through, there were small troops of Boy Scouts and veterans of the Great War, standing at attention in silence as the motors sped by. In the yards of factories and mills, workmen stood in groups, waiting. Men held their hats or caps to their hearts, women folded their hands. Farms and fields on the road had been tidied up, as a mark of respect, and at a place where carpenters were building a house they had cleared away the lumber and chips.

The rain stopped for a while. The mists that had drifted low over the mountains gave place to blue sky. White, straight birch trunks glistened, and ice began to melt in the sunshine. But as they drove on, deeper into the Green Mountain country, black clouds spread and rain fell again, harder. The red tail lights of the cars gleamed on the road in the wintry and dark afternoon.

When the cars reached the end of the journey, the skies lightened palely a moment. The burying ground was outside the village where the dead man was born. Generations of his ancestors had been laid to rest there, in graves on the hillside. The cars climbed the steep road and stopped. The family and a handful of friends got out and stood waiting.

Across the road, in a rocky field, the men and women of the village had gathered. They were not the kind of people to intrude or crowd nearer, and they kept complete silence. The young minister said a few words as the coffin was lowered. A sudden storm of hail pelted down.

The widow, who had tried to smile that morning coming out of the church, could no longer hold back her tears.

The cars left. The bent-shouldered sexton signalled to his helpers. They filled in the grave. Four country militiamen took up their positions on guard. Snow fell that night on the hillside and the slopes of Salt Ash Mountain.

The headstone that now marks the quiet spot bears no inscription but the name, Calvin Coolidge, the dates, and the President's seal.